Five Elements of
Collective Leadership
for Early Childhood
Professionals

"*Five Elements of Collective Leadership for Early Child Professionals* is a revolutionary manual, spelling out how leadership in any human endeavor needs to be redefined and reenacted as a collective rather than an individual activity. This single shift has the potential to reinvigorate stalled democracy and educate citizens in participatory democracy from the very outset."
—Mary Hartman, founder, Rutgers Global Institute for Women's Leadership

"As an early childhood professional, I'm always looking for opportunities to engage and collaborate with other community stakeholders to improve coordination of services for young children and families. Our amazing coalition known as the Santa Cruz Birth to Five Partners has been in existence since 2013 due in large part to what we've learned about collective leadership from Cassandra O'Neill. It's made all of the difference in the world."
—Francisco J. Padilla, regional director, Santa Cruz Regional Partnership Council, First Things First

"This book will change the way we think, discuss, and practice leadership in the field of early childhood education. It's a resource that will be used over and over again. Part literature review, part resource guide, part handbook, part conversation starter—100 percent insightful." —Elisa Mongeluzzi, MEd, early childhood coach, mentor, and advocate

"At this pivotal time in early childhood education, it's imperative that we develop systems built on diversity of thought, action, and leadership. This book offers a framework for reflection when leading change in your community, including real-life examples of how to put the beliefs into action."
—Amber Jones, early education and systems thinking consultant

"Relationships are crucial when guiding our students toward success. Done properly, these relationships form a complex and dynamic web between students, teachers, principals, families, and the community. *Five Elements of Collective Leadership for Early Childhood Professionals* is a valuable resource that focuses on the intentionality of building and maintaining the relationships that are critical to this process." —Mike MacEwan, MSM, educational consult and collaborative relationship builder

# Five Elements of Collective Leadership

## for Early Childhood Professionals

Cassandra O'Neill and Monica Brinkerhoff

Redleaf Press®
www.redleafpress.org
800-423-8309

Published by Redleaf Press
10 Yorkton Court
St. Paul, MN 55117
www.redleafpress.org

National Association for the
Education of Young Children
1313 L Street NW, Suite 500
Washington, DC 20005-4101
NAEYC.org

First edition 2017
Cover design by Jim Handrigan
Interior design by Erin Kirk New
Typeset in Adobe Minion Pro
Interior illustrations on page 80 by Jim Handrigan, 114 by Erin Kirk New
Printed in the United States of America
24  23  22  21  20  19  18  17     1  2  3  4  5  6  7  8

Library of Congress Cataloging-in-Publication Data

Names: O'Neill, Cassandra, author. | Brinkerhoff, Monica, author.
Title: Five elements of collective leadership for early childhood
    professionals / Cassandra O'Neill and Monica Brinkerhoff.
Description: First edition. | St. Paul, MN : Redleaf Press, [2018] | Includes
    bibliographical references and index.
Identifiers: LCCN 2017023635 (print) | LCCN 2017036599 (ebook) | ISBN
    9781605545479 (ebook) | ISBN 9781605545462 (pbk. : alk. paper)
Subjects: LCSH: Early childhood educators. | Early childhood education. |
    Leadership. | Educational leadership.
Classification: LCC LB1139.23 (ebook) | LCC LB1139.23 .O54 2018 (print)
    | DDC
    372.21—dc23
LC record available at https://lccn.loc.gov/2017023635

Printed on acid-free paper                          NAEYC Item 1133

To my parents, William L. O'Neill (1935–2016) and
E. Carol O'Neill. I appreciate all the support and love
they have given me during my life. I am grateful for
the curiosity, love of learning, creativity, and passion
for social justice that I got from them, which have
been the foundational values of my life and career.
—Cassandra

For my parents, Tom and Rose Burchett, who nurtured
both my sense of responsibility and adventure. Thank
you for believing in me and for providing a model of
continuous learning, strategic thinking, partnership,
collaboration, and most of all, love.
—Monica

# Contents

# Foreword

When I wrote *Doing the Right Thing for Children: Eight Qualities of Leadership* in 2014, there was a paucity of books that actually addressed leadership qualities, competencies, and practices within settings serving children from birth to age eight. The search for just right information that was a good fit for those who were current leaders, aspiring leaders, or students of leadership was long and arduous. It was a journey that required grit, perseverance, and tenacity.

The anthropological concept *cultural parallelism* is where two cultures evolve with similar practices, beliefs, and mores, although they exist in different physical locations and without evidence of interactions among the two. In reading the authors' inspiration for writing the book, I was reminded of cultural parallelism and how similar our searches for leadership have been. Without any prior consultation, verbal communications, or professional interactions, we've made the same ports of call along our leadership journeys. We have been shaped, informed, and inspired by the same gurus housed in the pantheon of progressive educational thought and transformational leadership, including Urie Bronfenbrenner's ecological systems theory, Paulo Freire's democratic and ethical pedagogy framework, Peter Senge's systems thinking approach, Saul Alinsky's rules for radicals, and finally Loris Malaguzzi's vision of the child. It appears that the authors and I have been looking through the same interdisciplinary, multidimensional lens for leadership substance and sustenance.

And now you, the readers of this book, are about to enjoy the benefits of Cassandra and Monica's leadership journey as they guide you through a thoughtful and useful explanation and application of collective leadership theory. They are clear and concise about its application and acknowledge that there is no magical combination that makes some leaders more successful than others. However, they show how having a leadership tool kit at your disposal that includes collective leadership increases your opportunities to maximize your team's contributions and efforts toward achieving your organization's desired results. They describe the pitfalls of having all the creative thinking, driving energy, and quantitative decision making vested in one individual. When using a collective approach, leadership is owned and operated by the whole organization. In other words, you cannot address organizational-based needs through individual-based responses.

I believe an essential leadership capability is knowledge: knowledge of self, knowledge of others, knowledge of craft, and knowledge of leadership. This book deepens our understanding of leadership by exposing us to its four core theories (trait theory, behavioral theory, contingency theory, and power and influence theory) while placing collective leadership within the appropriate domain of behavioral leadership.

So what follows, for your reading pleasure, is an awesome, just right book on leadership that will indeed be a good fit for those who are serious about how leadership can be practiced in early childhood settings.

Maurice Sykes
*Doing the Right Thing for Children: Eight Qualities of Leadership*

# Acknowledgments

As with any book, so many people have contributed that there aren't enough pages to list them all. We have been privileged to work with each other and the early childhood education community in Arizona for the last ten years, Cassandra as a consultant and Monica in various roles in early childhood settings. We appreciate the opportunity to deepen our learning about how to help individuals (and the field as a whole) and develop the capacity to reach shared goals through collective leadership. Specifically, we want to thank LaVonne Douville, Naomi Karp, and Allison Titcomb from the United Way of Tucson and Southern Arizona for their inspiration and leadership in the Tucson community. We also want to acknowledge staff from Arizona's quality rating and improvement system, Quality First. We learned together with people from First Things First, Valley of the Sun United Way, and coaches and coach supervisors from the organizations working with the Quality First program. We especially want to thank Jill Morgan for her inspirational and intentional leadership while we worked on Quality First. Thanks to all who have worked to increase the quality of early childhood programs and services and have been willing to try new things, give us feedback, and share their challenges and triumphs in building collective leadership with each other and with those they coach. We have benefited greatly from learning with these groups and individuals.

We are grateful to other consultants we have worked with whose time, thoughts, and guidance were appreciated, including Mary Bouley, Jim Roussin, Judi Gottschalk, and Sarah Griffiths. And we appreciate all those whom we interviewed for this book, who filled out the survey we created to capture examples from the field, who looked at our outlines and drafts, and who provided feedback, support, and advice, including

Stacie Goffin, Rhian Evans Allvin, Amber Jones, Angie Cole, and Tracy Benson.

Finally, many thanks to our editor, Andrea Rud, whose patience, guidance, eye for detail, and collaboration helped us reach the finish line of this project. We would also like to thank Kara Lomen and the staff at Redleaf Press, who provided the spark of inspiration for this book.

# Introduction

Go to the people. Live with them. Learn from them. Love them. Start with what they know. Build with what they have. But with the best leaders, when the work is done, the task accomplished, the people will say, "We have done this ourselves."
—Lao-tzu

How can everyone most powerfully pursue a purpose that transcends us all? Together we have been thinking about this question for years. We have worked together for ten years with early childhood leaders and professionals in Arizona: Monica as a practitioner and Cassandra as a consultant and coach. During our work, we sensed that it was time to do things differently. From the context of the early childhood field, to the ever-increasing attention to complex problems that face society, to the voices of the teachers, coaches, and administrators with whom we worked, a common theme emerged: it is time to rethink how we work together, how we inspire and sustain change, and most of all, how we think about leadership.

We were drawn to each other because of our shared value system: people are inherently capable, and the change process should be focused on developing strengths and building capacity; what people and groups often need most is time and space to build awareness and articulate what they already know so they can take steps to do what they know needs to be done; and adult learning and change should be focused on principals of engagement. Over the years, we applied this value system to our work together—sometimes explicitly and sometimes implicitly. We have experimented with the strategies and practices outlined in this book while delivering workshops, coaching, supporting communities of practice, developing leadership, facilitating meetings and retreats, and evaluating programs. As a result, we have been colearners in promoting collective leadership and helping people and groups realize their fullest potential. We believe that to truly meet the goals of our field, there must be shared leadership among the people within systems and within our field—at every level. These goals belong to us all, and it is only through working in collaboration that they can be accomplished.

Why do we believe collective leadership is the next step in the evolution of our profession? Here are our stories.

## Cassandra

I have been interested in shared leadership my entire career, and practiced it without knowing what it was called since my first job after college. The job was to run a leadership program at a women's college for students interested in politics and public policy. My first step was to have a meeting to ask the students what they wanted to learn and what they were interested in. The group brainstormed multiple topics, and then I designed the semester's workshops around those topics. Thinking back, no one told me to do it this way; it just seemed like a natural thing to do. As I got further along in my career, I continued to be interested in getting ideas and feedback from people I was working with—especially when planning to meet their needs. However, it became harder and harder to work this way while working in organizations with rigid job descriptions and hierarchical, top-down decision making.

Everything changed when I learned about coaching. I learned there were engaging ways to facilitate meetings and retreats. I learned methods that were designed to help people hear from each other in meaningful ways and work together toward shared goals instead of having goals imposed on them by others. I realized that what I was learning was something I had been aware of before. But now I was learning intentional methods to help people grow and develop, become more self-directed (rather than other-directed), and thrive as a result of the growth that was happening. It occurred to me that while I didn't know what it was called, I had already been doing these very same things, both as a high school student when I taught swimming lessons and tutored younger students in math and in my first job. But after years in the workforce, I had unlearned these approaches and learned less-effective but more-expected or conventional ways of working. Now, finally, I had a name for how to work differently with people, and I had a tool kit to use to intentionally build shared leadership and help people connect meaningfully with their shared aspirations and dreams. I was so excited about this that I began to use these approaches whenever I could and to teach them to as many people as were interested.

I began to hear about collective leadership, sometimes also called shared leadership or distributed leadership, and to incorporate it into my work with early childhood programs, schools, nonprofits, coalitions, and funders. In 2008 the book *Forces for Good: The Six Practices of High-Impact Nonprofits* came out and listed shared leadership as one of the six practices of high-impact nonprofits. This research identified how sharing leadership across people in an organization was critical to having high impact and being sustainable, an often-elusive goal for organizations. Having worked for years with organizations that were limited in achieving their stated goals, I was noticing some common patterns. First, the ways staff were treated and often how families served by professionals were treated were not consistent with or conducive to the strengths-based work so often touted by decision makers. Second, organizations were often chasing elusive funding, which led to starting and stopping programs without any sustainability. Successive and significant budget cuts beginning in 2008 and, for many, continuing to this day led to staff feeling depleted and disempowered. Most were given instructions to do more with less—and at the same time empower the children and families they served. I often sat in meetings wondering "How are they going to do that when they themselves are not feeling powerful?"

I noticed that the people at the top of hierarchies were often baffled why staff members weren't responding better to the mandates they were receiving. This was similar to the joke that the flogging will continue until morale improves. And the same people in leadership positions were often convinced that their staff or the children and families they served were the problem rather than the source of the solution.

## Monica

I started to think about collective leadership, though I had no name for it, as a child care center director in the late 1990s. In my role, I continued to study the principles of the Reggio Emilia approach to early childhood education, with the ultimate goal of incorporating the ideas and principles into our program. One of the things I most appreciated about the Reggio approach was the foundational value that children are competent learners. I also connected with the idea of establishing a classroom community where the children were part of creating classroom rules and norms, and where the curriculum followed the strengths and interests of the children. Today these ideas are well accepted as best practice in our field (Lewin-Benham 2011), but at that time, they were considered innovative. Some of the teachers at our center were interested in applying the Reggio learning principles to their teaching practice, so we did a lot of thinking together about how to implement the new ideas and approaches into our existing learning philosophy. Additionally, as a somewhat new director, I was in the process of immersing myself in leadership books and articles, both from the business world and the early childhood education field. I started to wonder whether the principles we were trying to use in the classroom might be applied to leadership and adult learning.

Around the same time, I returned to school to work toward a graduate degree in social work. As I continued to learn more about how systems influence people (Bronfenbrenner 1992), strategies for community engagement and organizing (Alinsky 1971; Freire 1970), and strengths-based practice, I continued to build a foundation of theoretical knowledge that would later support my ability to embrace the idea of collective leadership.

In 2009 I was exposed to some ideas that could be considered life changing in a professional sense. I attended a systems thinking seminar based on the thoughts and ideas of Peter Senge and a course on coaching in education. This is also when I met Cassandra; she was the trainer for the coach training. Around the same time, I worked for a nonprofit agency that was leading a collaborative process to try to replicate a Promise Neighborhood in Tucson, Arizona. We used a collective impact approach and implemented ideas used by others across the United States who were using cross-sector collaboration to solve complex social issues. These foundations and frameworks deepened my sense of and curiosity about how these ideas might support leaders in the early childhood care and education field.

Our field is addressing complex social change. Increasingly we are integral parts of cross-sector initiatives, and we are even creating our own systems that require a new level of collaboration, such as quality rating and improvement systems. More often than not, we find ourselves working in collaboration with colleagues from other fields, engaging in processes that involve multiple partners, and designing systems that integrate several sectors. Paired with a new emphasis from funders (private and public alike) on the value of collaboration, these conditions require from us a new skill set that will allow us to make connections, work flexibly, and navigate increasing complexity and change. This is no easy task and certainly not one that any one person or team can do alone.

## Who Is This Book For?

We have written this book to help readers think differently about the way they lead, whether they are teachers, providers, administrators, or systems change leaders. If you want to explore ways to lead your classroom, team, organization, or coalition in a way that allows all voices to be heard, provides a more equitable distribution of power, utilizes the gifts of all members, and engages everyone in a common vision, this book is for you.

## What You Will Find in This Book

In chapter 1, we will discuss leadership in the early childhood education context, explain the concept of collective leadership, and compare it to "traditional" leadership approaches. We will also discuss the development of collective leadership based on our own research and foundational works written by others on this topic.

Chapter 2 will outline how changes in the world and in our field warrant a new kind of leadership. We will also describe why we think collective leadership is a perfect match for the field of early childhood education and invite you to think about what a new approach to leadership might look like to you in your own role.

In chapter 3, we will discuss the foundation of collective leadership: trust. We will explore how the very real dynamics of power, privilege, and inequity affect trust and collective leadership. We will also provide a few resources to help surface assumptions about power and privilege and begin dialogue about these dynamics to allow your group to find common ground.

Chapter 4 will provide a description of the five elements of collective leadership: Shared Vision and Reenvisioning, Wholeness, Collective Wisdom/Intelligence, Coaction, and Evolution/Emergence. We will explain each element, the core value related to each element, and the belief that underlies each element. This section will also outline what the element might look like in practice, as well as introduce some tools and practices that are helpful in using the ideas in this book.

In chapter 5, we will provide examples of what collective leadership looks like when it is used in early childhood education (ECE) settings and will describe how it might be used with families; in the role of a teacher, family care provider, home visitor, center director, manager, supervisor, administrator, coach, consultant, mentor, or technical assistance provider; in professional development, goverance, networks, coalitions, and systems change; and as a funder. This chapter also includes stories of people in the ECE field who are already using these ideas in these roles.

Chapter 6 will provide you with a few things to consider as you are beginning your collective leadership journey, including common challenges and some ideas to address them.

Chapter 7 includes case studies describing how an organization and a statewide partnership are using collective leadership.

And, finally, the appendix provides a list of resources to continue your exploration of collective leadership, as well as tools you can use to help you implement collective leadership ideas.

## What You Will Not Find in This Book

You will not find a recipe to "do" collective leadership. The tools and ideas in this book are for you to use in your own unique way, to apply to your unique and individual context. Collective leadership is like jazz—it is a process of engagement and improvisation. Collective leadership, as we will explain later, is not a script of steps. Rather, it is a journey that you and your group (team, coaching partner, coalition) will embark upon. The journey will require patience, courage, and trust, and will inevitably have its ups and downs. But as with any epic journey, there will be potential for deep learning, meaningful engagement, and transformation. And after all, isn't that what we are all striving to create for children and families?

# What Is Collective Leadership?

What is collective leadership? How does it compare to a more traditional concept of leadership? Why would anyone want to use it? What are the benefits? How did it develop and what are its theoretical foundations? In this chapter, we answer these questions.

## What Collective Leadership Is and Isn't

We have defined collective leadership as a group of people working together toward a shared goal (Brinkerhoff, Murrieta, and O'Neill 2015). When collective leadership is happening, people are internally and externally motivated, working together toward a shared vision within a group, and using their unique talents and skills to contribute to the success. In fact, collective leadership recognizes that lasting success is not possible without diverse perspectives and contributions.

Collective leadership is a process. It is dependent on the relationships among the parts in the system, whether that system is two people working together; a classroom, team, or organization; or a system initiative. In collective leadership, the way the group works together makes it different from a more traditional model of leadership. How the group works together and the unique results that are possible only when this happens differentiate a group that is sharing leadership from one that is not.

In collective leadership, there is shared responsibility and decision making, accountability, and authentic engagement. All members are involved in creating the vision and are committed to working to achieve that vision. Collective leadership is based on the assumption that everyone *can* and *should* lead (Preskill and Brookfield 2009). Collective leadership requires specific conditions for the success of the whole: trust, shared power, transparent and effective communication, accountability, and shared learning. It is based on the recognition that without the gifts, talents, perspectives, and efforts of many, sustainable change is difficult to achieve. Creativity is unleashed as people tap into their fullest abilities and capacities. When collective leadership is present, people say, "We have done this ourselves."

A key aspect of collective leadership is that the success depends on the leadership within the entire group rather than the skills of one person. Mary Parker Follett, whom we consider to be the mother of collective leadership, wrote about power *with* others rather than power *over* others (Fox and Urwick 1973). This means that rather than having leadership limited to one charismatic person or one powerful organization, leadership is shared among many. This shift from focusing on the skills of any one individual to the capacities, relationships, behaviors, and practices of an entire group (two or more people) makes collective leadership different from other types of leadership and leadership models.

In "Leadership in the Age of Complexity," Margaret Wheatley and Debbie Frieze (2010) discuss a shift from thinking of a leader as a "hero" to thinking of a leader as a "host." When a leader is the "hero," he or she is expected to have all the answers, solve all the problems, and fix everything for everyone else. The "hero" is dynamic, charismatic, and brilliant. The problem with this mind-set is that the command and control model often uses quick solutions that are created by a few in power (the top of an organizational chart), and often these solutions are not well suited for the complex issues that we face today. Instead, we need leaders as "hosts": those who have the skills to promote shared learning, effective group decision making, reflection, visioning and goal setting, and mutual accountability.

What does this shift from "hero" to "host" look like? The following table shows some of the key differences between traditional and collective leadership.

## Comparison of Traditional and Collective Leadership

|  | Traditional leadership | Collective leadership |
| --- | --- | --- |
| View of organizations | Organizations as machines | Organizations as systems |
| Structure | Hierarchy, pyramid | Connected networks |
| Decision making | Top-down | Shared and/or rotated |
| Assumptions about people's capacity | People need to be told what to do | People are inherently capable and can be trusted to do the right thing |
| Beliefs about how success is created | One person has the skill or talent to create success | Success comes from the diverse perspectives and skills of many |

### Perceptions of Leadership

When we have introduced the topic of collective leadership to groups, sometimes very few hands raise in response to the question, "Who has heard of collective leadership?" However, when we explain more about what it is, it begins to sound familiar to some people who have been thinking about the issue of developing leadership both within individuals and across teams and groups. To others, it is very different from how they have thought about leadership before. What we are calling "collective leadership" has also been described as shared leadership and distributed leadership. We chose the term *collective leadership* when we began our adoption of this approach, in part because one of the seminal works that guided our initial learning and thinking on the topic was *The Collective Leadership Framework* by the W. K. Kellogg Foundation (2007).

It is sometimes easier to talk about what collective leadership isn't than what it is. When we ask a group to name some old ideas about leadership, people say things such as "top-down," "hierarchy," "people at the top make decisions, create a vision, and tell others what to do." When we ask people for some new ideas about leadership, they talk about shared decision making and getting input from a variety of people affected by decisions. As we explore this topic, you will find that there are many ways to develop collective leadership, and there are many ways it can be used.

## Mental Models about Leadership

Mental models are deeply held beliefs about the world around us that often shape how we think and behave. Another way to think about mental models is as assumptions. Mental models are usually hidden under the surface, just like an iceberg—if you aren't aware they are there, they can cause damage. Before you read any further, we invite you to uncover your own mental models of leadership. Reflect on the following questions:

What first comes to your mind when you think of a leader?
What are some life events or prior experiences that helped shape that mental model?
What does leadership mean to you? How is it the same as or different than managing, supervising, or directing?
What do you think it means to lead?
Who can be a leader?
How do you want others to see your leadership? Or what do you want others to say about you as a leader?

## Benefits of Collective Leadership

Collective leadership has many benefits, most resulting from the fact that you get better results from considering multiple perspectives, sharing responsibility, building upon the strengths of those on your team, and leveraging internal motivation. The following are some specific benefits you might expect to see when collective leadership is in action.

*Better Decisions and Increased Effectiveness*
A major benefit is that work is more effective and impactful when there is collective leadership. When people at the top make decisions that affect others without a chance to get input and multiple perspectives, the decisions often aren't as effective as when multiple perspectives are considered. When those who will be affected by the decisions have a

chance to provide feedback, ideas, and even direction, the decisions are much more likely to be effective, because leaders have considered the perspectives of many, not just those at the top.

### Increased Self-Direction and Motivation

Common challenges faced by managers are related to people resisting a change or directive. What if there was a way to easily motivate your team so they were able to generate their own solutions and work toward their own growth and development? There is! Just as we encourage young children to be internally motivated and to adopt a "growth mind-set" (Galinsky 2010; Dweck 2006), managers or others who are leading change efforts can help those around them be internally motivated. As we know is true for young children, internal motivation is much more powerful than external motivation. Those who respond to their own internal drives, interests, desires, and motivations are much more likely to work toward and sustain change than those who are externally motivated by "carrots and sticks" (Pink 2009).

What is needed for adult growth and development are for barriers to internal motivation to be removed. Early childhood programs are designed to prepare children to be independent, self-motivated, and active learners. If the adults working in these programs are not acting the same way, it's hard for them to facilitate children's development. And if the adults who are supervising, mentoring, or coaching others are not seeking to grow and develop these early childhood professionals, there is a real limit to what is possible. Imposing change onto someone else creates resistance. All the effort from people who feel they are being told they are not doing a good job goes into defending themselves, which often looks like resistance to the people trying to "help" them. Instead, if we spend time developing relationships and finding out what others' goals and wishes are, it is possible to form a partnership to work together toward a shared goal.

In "The Neuroscience of Leadership," David Rock and Jeffrey Schwartz (2006) describe the architecture of the brain that contributes to this phenomenon:

> For insights to be useful, they need to be generated from within, not given to individuals as conclusions. This is true for several reasons. First, people will experience the adrenaline-like rush of insight only if they go through the process of making connections themselves. The moment of insight is well known to be a positive and energizing experience. This rush of energy

may be central to facilitating change: It helps fight against the internal (and external) forces trying to keep change from occurring, including the fear response of the amygdala.

Second, neural networks are influenced moment to moment by genes, experiences, and varying patterns of attention. Although all people have some broad functions in common, in truth everyone has a unique brain architecture. Human brains are so complex and individual that there is little point in trying to work out how another person ought to reorganize his or her thinking. It is far more effective and efficient to help others come to their own insights. Accomplishing this feat requires self-observation. Adam Smith, in his 1759 masterpiece *The Theory of Moral Sentiments*, referred to this as being "the spectators of our own behavior."

### Shared Responsibility

In traditional models, the few people at the top often feel burdened and alone. These managers and supervisors often feel like everyone is turning to them for answers, and the pressure is exhausting. When responsibility is shared, managers feel like they are surrounded by resourceful people. And distributing the responsibility they have with others is a relief. Those at the bottom of the hierarchy are often underutilized, with an unfulfilled desire to contribute more. They are hungry for more responsibility. When the responsibility is shared, the work is easier and more fun for everyone involved!

### Realizing Potential

Too often, people do not get to realize their potential at work. This is especially limiting in the field of early childhood education, as a key purpose of education is to help children reach their fullest potential. Adopting a collective leadership approach helps people grow and develop not only in their current jobs and job responsibilities, but also as professionals. In his book *Drive*, Daniel Pink (2009) writes that people are motivated by autonomy, purpose, and mastery. This means that people are most motivated when they feel trusted to make decisions and develop solutions, when they feel connected to the purpose of their work, and when they can do things that are challenging and that help them grow and develop. Allowing people opportunities to develop mastery, align with purpose, and increase autonomy increases motivation and satisfaction. It also allows people to develop new skills and talents that could allow them to contribute more through their current positions and may lead to advances in their careers.

### Increased Engagement and Investment

When leadership is shared and cultivated, people are more engaged, energized, and invested in the goals. This happens because people have a sense of ownership of the goals: they helped create them, so they are much more invested in seeing them come to life.

### Sustainability

Sustainability is often elusive without collective leadership. If everything is dependent on one person and that person leaves, what happens? Work grinds to a halt, or the person's absence results in missing knowledge and information that are difficult to recover. In contrast, where there is collective leadership, knowledge, responsibility, and information are shared across a group.

Another aspect of sustainability is to sustain a change or improvement. Take the example of quality-improvement initiatives (or quality rating and improvement systems), in which the quality of early childhood programs is the focus of change. If the change is directed by someone other than the teacher or staff, it is less likely to be continued. In contrast, when the change is driven by a partnership between the teacher and whoever is leading or supporting/directing the change, the change is much more likely to be sustained. In this dynamic of "power with" versus "power over," the teacher is actively involved in a collaborative partnership and is part of leading the change process. According to Senge, Hamilton, and Kania (2015, 29), "Ineffective leaders try to make change happen. System leaders focus on creating the conditions that can produce change and that can eventually cause change to be self-sustaining."

## Misperceptions about Collective Leadership

It's important to keep in mind a few common misperceptions about collective leadership. First, some believe that collective leadership means that there are no leaders and that the group, effort, or organization is "leaderless." This is not the case. Instead, collective leadership is "leaderful," meaning that the leadership capacity of the members of the group is realized (Raelin 2003). In leaderful organizations, efforts, and groups, everyone has a chance to exhibit leadership, leadership occurs at every level, and individuals are willing to set aside their individual agendas to pursue the group's goals and interests. The leadership capacity of the group as a whole (or the entire system) is also present in leaderful settings. In contrast to the notion that collective leadership means that there are no leaders, collective leadership actually means that leadership is abundant and thriving at all levels.

Another misperception is that we often tend to interchange the concepts of "leader" and "leadership." In other words, we tend to think that "leadership" is something that a leader does. In this view, the "hero" leader enters the picture and "leads" the group, providing the actions and solutions and plans. Instead, complexity leadership theory provides another way to look at it: leadership is a *process* that is both interactive and emergent (Uhl-Bien, Marion, and McKelvey 2007). From this perspective, leaders are those who act in ways that influence positive outcomes and engage in an interactive and emergent process. Leadership is a set of interactions rather than actions of an individual. Traditional leadership theory has focused more on the actions of individuals. Instead, we invite you to think about leadership itself as systems and processes. In collective leadership, leadership is like a living organism in and of itself, and all members are considered leaders as they participate in the process of growing and developing that living organism.

Even when collective leadership is present, there are times when individual leadership is needed. The image of a teeter-totter is helpful to show that balance is needed between collective and individual leadership. For example, to make collective leadership effective, structure and organization need to be in place. This means that, at times, individuals will need to demonstrate what we might consider to be "leader behaviors": facilitating a meeting, reminding the group of their prior agreements and systems for accountability, and sometimes even giving direction. Just as there is not a one-size-fits-all approach in the classroom, neither is there an either/or distinction between collective leadership and individual leadership. It is not all or nothing. We need both individual and collective leadership. Sometimes you may need to be directive, and other times you may need to be directed by others—and there will also be times when it will be in between.

It's also hard to talk about leadership and leading without the term *followers* coming up. What first comes to mind when you think of a follower? Most people have a somewhat negative connotation. The term *follower* connotes that people are not thinking on their own or at all and are not contributing. It connotes a passive behavior—as if they were lemmings. We don't want lemmings! Instead, we can recognize that sometimes people are "following," but that doesn't make them "followers." Take the example of geese: they fly in V formation and take turns in the lead position. Dr. Robert McNeish (1972) is credited with comparing leadership to how geese fly in formation. The geese are interdependent, and all have the capacity to fly at the front. Another way to think about this is provided by Nancy Duarte and Patti Sanchez (2016), who call people "travelers." Sometimes a few people do need to hold a vision for a group and help the group travel toward it. However, leading does not necessarily mean telling others what to do. Leading may mean directing, it may mean listening, and it may mean helping people think through a situation.

In practice, you will probably use a combination of individual and collective leadership. This is a good thing. Remember: it doesn't have to be all or nothing. As Arthur Costa and Robert Garmston (2002, 19) write, "We need great teams, and we need great individuals. Teamwork can take us only so far; then we need individual greatness. Individual greatness can take us only so far; then we need team greatness. Team and individual are not separate and distinct concepts. They are in dynamic relationship, merged organically into one whole."

## Development of Collective Leadership

Authors describing collective leadership agree that the reason this approach to leadership is so timely is that we now face complex problems (Cheung and Grubb 2014; Senge, Hamilton, and Kania 2015). In particular, knowledge workers are increasingly challenged to adapt to situations and problems that often emerge over time and do not have a clear course of action or solution (Meehan and Reinelt 2012). Anyone who has been a coach, an administrator, or a teacher in an early education setting can attest to the fact that many of the daily challenges we face are not simple and don't have a simple solution. Traditional models of leadership highlight the skills and capabilities of an individual, but to effectively address the challenges we now face, we need to move beyond a focus on the individual and toward the collective (Kuenkel and Schaefer 2013).

When did the idea of collective leadership emerge, and where did it come from? Collective leadership is very similar to the concepts of shared leadership, democratic leadership, emergent leadership, and distributed leadership (Bolden 2011). In *Shared Leadership: Reframing the Hows and Whys of Leadership*, Craig Pearce and Jay Conger (2003) write that alternatives to the traditional concept of command and control leadership emerged in the early twentieth century. As evidence, they write that in 1924, Mary Parker Follett introduced the idea of the law of the situation, which suggested that instead of following the lead of the official authority in any given situation, people should follow the person with the most knowledge of the situation at hand. This was a much different idea of leadership than what was generally accepted at the time. Because of Follett's ideas about education, leadership, and community engagement, we consider her to be the mother of collective leadership.

Over the next seventy years, there were many contributions to leadership and management theory that helped lay the groundwork for collective leadership, but it wasn't until the late 1990s that scholars returned to the idea of shared leadership in organizations (Pearce and Conger 2003).

Collective leadership has been used in a variety of fields, including community development, health care, educational leadership, environmental sustainability and science, nonprofit management, and even the military. Clearly, this cross-sector approach to a reimagined leadership approach holds promise for our field.

### Teal Organizations: Collective Leadership and Self-Direction, Wholeness, and Evolutionary Purpose

In 2014 Frederic Laloux's book *Reinventing Organizations: A Guide to Creating Organizations Inspired by the Next Stage of Human Consciousness* was published, and a worldwide conversation began about organizations that were operating out of what Laloux calls the "next stage of human consciousness." He created a developmental scale based on the literature about the developmental stages of human consciousness. The level or stage of human consciousness of the people founding, owning, and leading organizations determines the structures and practices in an organization. Laloux assigns the color orange to the level of the traditional hierarchical organizational structure and teal to organizations operating from a consciousness exhibiting a different approach to leadership.

Teal organizations utilize practices in three areas: wholeness, self-management, and evolutionary purpose. These practices are the breakthroughs from earlier levels of consciousness. The metaphor for teal organizations is that of a living system, compared with the machine metaphor for orange. Although Laloux doesn't use the term *collective leadership*, teal organizations are being operated from a collective leadership model.

Research has shown that self-managed teams are more successful and effective than "boss"-driven teams. Daniel Pink has popularized the social science research showing that the internal motivators of purpose, mastery, and autonomy are much more powerful than external motivators (carrot and stick approaches). Laloux's *Reinventing Organizations* described in detail how twelve teal organizations operated, giving information about the different ways to design and implement next-stage organizations by adopting teal practices, including self-managing teams.

It may be harder to adopt some of the teal practices in government agencies, schools, and organizations with civil-service systems based on rigid job descriptions and rules that often limit or prevent self-management and other practices that lead to wholeness than it would be in businesses. But educators can adopt collective leadership. One of the organizations Laloux profiled is a teal school in Berlin that has self-managing students, teachers, and parents. The school called ESBZ is a grade 7–12 school that has adopted the following practices:

- Students are given full responsibility for their learning, teaching themselves and each other.
- Tutor-teachers are mentors and coaches; they offer encouragement, counsel, praise, feedback, and challenge.
- Students self-pace their learning, learn on their own, or form small groups.
- Students meet one-on-one with their tutor-teacher to review their logbook, which records their accomplishments.
- Teachers self-manage; they form teams that work together and can make most decisions without needing approval from the principal.
- Parents self-manage by volunteering three hours per month.
- Workshops are given regularly to principals and teachers who want to learn more about how the school works—these are taught by students. (Laloux 2014)

Luckily, adopting collective leadership practices is not an all-or-nothing proposition. Managers and leaders can begin to move toward what we are calling "collective leadership" and what Laloux calls "going teal." We believe that for the field of early childhood education to reach its stated goals, professionals must move toward collective leadership at every level—organization, program, team, coach, teacher, and family. Although collective leadership is being used by some, our field can accelerate it through intentionality. We can look for ways to do this in our daily work, whether we are teaching children, coaching teachers, or working in networks, coalitions, or collective impact initiatives. The way in which we are working toward quality and educational goals is just as important (if not more so) than what is being achieved along the way.

## The Dawn of Systems Leadership: Senge, Hamilton, and Kania

In 2015 an article related to collective leadership written by Peter Senge, Hal Hamilton, and John Kania was published in the *Stanford Social Innovation Review*. In it they describe a systems leader as the type of leader needed for successful system-change initiatives: "At no time in history have we needed such systems leaders more. We face a host of systemic challenges beyond the reach of existing institutions and their hierarchical authority structures" (28). Senge, Hamilton, and Kania describe competencies (which they call "capabilities") and strategies for those who want to become system leaders. Systems leaders are described as those who can see the bigger picture and entire system, foster reflection and learning, and shift the focus of a group from solving problems to "co-creating the future" (29). These skills are the same skills needed to successfully lead an early childhood program, organization, or initiative. This article is important to the development and application of collective leadership in that it connects ideas that are foundational to collective impact and systems thinking and applies them to leadership.

## Collective Impact and Systems Building

One of our favorite resources on collective leadership is *The Collective Leadership Framework* (W. K. Kellogg Foundation 2007). This framework outlines an approach to community development grounded in principles of collective leadership, with a goal to enable communities and organizations to create sustainable and systemic change. In this framework, organizations begin with building relationships around a shared purpose. Once a clear plan is developed with systems for accountability, communication, and roles based on talents and passion, the work is done with regular opportunities for reflection and learning. Adaptations are made as necessary for overall success, and in this way, the work emerges—an intentional yet responsive and organic process.

Four years after *The Collective Leadership Framework* was published, the *Stanford Social Innovation Review* published an article on a concept called "collective impact" (Kania and Kramer 2011). As Collaboration for Impact (2017) defines it, collective impact is "a framework to tackle deeply entrenched and complex social problems. It is an innovative and structured approach to making collaboration work across government, business, philanthropy, nonprofit organizations and citizens to achieve significant and lasting social change." How are collective impact and collective leadership connected? We see collective impact as the application of collective leadership at the systems-change level.

Kania and Kramer outlined conditions for large-scale systems change through collaboration among multiple organizations working toward shared community goals. In the article, the authors highlighted several examples of initiatives that were successfully using a collective impact approach to social change.

One of the featured initiatives was Strive, a "cradle to career" initiative that began in Cincinnati and is now being implemented nationally. Strive brought together leaders in Cincinnati to improve education and improve student success in multiple indicators across three large school districts. According to Kania and Kramer (2011), the initiative had positive impacts on high school graduation rates, fourth-grade reading and math scores, and the number of preschool children prepared for kindergarten, among others. This success occurred because the community leaders set aside their individual agendas and instead participated in a collective approach.

After the article was released, a national dialogue about collective impact began. A movement emerged that focused on helping and encouraging organizations to think beyond their own boundaries to solve complex and large challenges to create success through partnering or collaborating with other organizations. Collective impact approaches to community change brought to the forefront the fact that to create the kind of large-scale, sustainable change that is the goal of many funders and organizations alike, a collective approach is necessary.

Recently, the article "Collective Impact 3.0: An Evolving Framework for Community Change" (Cabaj and Weaver 2016) described the next level of development for such large-scale work. The authors suggest the framework is evolving, with experience and learning informing the work, and have suggested a revision to the leadership paradigm and conditions of collective impact originally set forth by Kania and Kramer. From Kania and Kramer's five conditions—common agenda, shared measurement, mutually reinforcing activities, continuous communication, and a backbone organization—Cabaj and Weaver (2016) suggest community aspiration, strategic learning, high-leverage activities, inclusive community engagement, and organizations as a container for change. This "evolution" of collective impact aligns with our understanding of collective leadership as evolving and focusing on both organizational advancement and movement building.

## Foundations for This Book

We developed the five elements of collective leadership outlined in chapter 4 after reviewing and connecting the ideas from a number of articles, books, and other resources, including those described above. We found commonalities among all and developed the five elements based on those common features. Our goal was to provide a useful framework for early childhood education leaders interested in using collective leadership in their settings. We recognize that these are not necessarily new ideas to some in our field. In fact, the ideas in this book are aligned with the foundational values and beliefs of ECE. What we have tried to do in this book is provide a framework and a name for many strategies already being used by many. We believe that this framework will support more intentional use of the strategies fieldwide. We also hope that this book builds a bridge for more early childhood education practitioners to connect to ideas and concepts used in other fields, such as organizational development and community development.

## Reflection: What Do You Know about Collective Leadership?

Now that you know more about collective leadership, how it has developed, and some of its theoretical foundations, we invite you to take a moment to reflect on the following questions:

Have you experienced collective leadership in the past? What was happening? How did you feel?

How is the idea of leadership as a process similar to or different from your own ideas about leadership?

What do you think are some things you might see in a "leadership journey"? What would group members be doing? How would they interact?

What do you think would be some important things for a group to keep in mind as they participated in a leadership process?

How do you feel about your own leadership potential when you consider leadership as a process rather than a skill, gift, or talent that one "leader" holds?

What opportunities do you see to use collective leadership in your work now?

# Collective Leadership in ECE: Why and Why Now?

Early childhood education today is affected by many forces for change coming from both outside and inside the field. In this chapter, we will discuss these forces, the benefits of collective leadership for the field of early childhood education in responding to these forces, some current field-level leadership initiatives, and how collective leadership fits into these efforts.

## Responding to External Forces

Some of the forces driving change are outside the ECE field and affect multiple sectors, communities, institutions, and even the world. We will highlight a few that we believe are especially important to the ECE field.

### Brain and Neuroscience Research

Advances in brain and neuroscience research have produced findings that place urgency on reaching children as early as possible. Research clearly connects early experiences with outcomes later in life. Additionally, research on adult development has helped us realize that adults can grow and develop in ways not previously thought possible. Taken together, these advances provide a prime opportunity to build upon what research tells us about adult growth, development, and change to maximize the quality of experiences and outcomes for young children.

Collective leadership aligns with recent findings related to neuroscience and what we are learning about adult development to truly engage adults in change and improvement, increase their motivation toward their work, and consider themselves responsible and accountable for movement toward shared goals. In "The Neuroscience of Leadership," David Rock and Jeffrey Schwartz (2006) explain that over the last three decades, scientists have been able to combine psychology with neuroscience and gain a much more accurate understanding of behavior change. Leaders and managers who understand the physiological nature of the brain and how it affects adults' ability to change behavior will be more successful in their change efforts and in reaching goals, achieving what Rock and Schwartz call "mindful change."

The strategies outlined in this book are aligned with the most recent findings about adult brain development, similar to those described by Rock and Schwartz. We have combined information from a variety of contemporary authors related to adults' growth, development, and change in our framework for collective leadership.

## Pressure on the Field by State and Federal Initiatives and Requirements and by Funders

There is pressure on the ECE field to change, grow, improve, adapt, and be accountable at all levels of our system. Increased public awareness of and attention on the field of ECE has provided necessary momentum for efforts to increase the quality of early experiences. Quality rating and improvement systems (QRIS) are just one example. In addition, the recognition of our field's history of fragmentation has resulted in efforts to combine and align across communities, systems, departments, and groups. For example, recent funding for Early Head Start–Child Care Partnerships combines the efforts of the Office of Child Care with the Office of Head Start, both under the United States Department of Health and Human Services Administration for Children and Families. This is an important change, as it signals a new level of collaboration and connection at the funder level.

New state and federal initiatives and funding bring additional requirements from both public and private funders. This is a good thing—it means that systems for accountability are being strengthened and developed so we can live up to our promise of improving outcomes for all children. It also means that for some programs, there has been an increase in reporting, grant applications, data collection and analysis, and other grant requirements, such as working with a quality-improvement coach. For some programs, these changes cause an increase in the amount of day-to-day work. Program administrators have the choice to try to carry this burden alone, which might result in higher levels of stress and less time for reflective and strategic thinking. Or they can choose to engage their teams and others around them in sharing in the responsibility. Policy makers can make decisions regarding grant requirements and funding based on what they think is the best course of action, or they can choose to gather input from those affected by the decisions to explore possible "unintended consequences" of policies.

When change initiatives are top-down and implemented without a spirit of partnership, the people working directly with children and families can feel like they are being burdened with requirements and demands. Collective leadership promotes opportunities for those doing the direct work to provide input into the development of the policies that directly affect their work and ability to be successful. Collective leadership can help all of us respond to new collaborations, policies, and requirements.

## Changes in Technology and a Global Economy

Advances in technology and the shifting global economy have created changes in what skills are needed for future generations as well as for the leaders of today. The world is changing around us, and we need to change in kind or become obsolete. If you have noticed that your work environment has become more complex and fast paced, you are not alone.

In a white paper titled *Future Trends in Leadership Development*, Nick Petrie (2014) writes that we are now in an environment that is fundamentally different from years past. We are in a period of rapid change, increasing complexity, and uncertainty. He describes an IBM study of over 1,500 CEOs that found that their top concerns were the growing complexity of their environments and that their organizations were not equipped to manage this increased level of complexity.

What trends are affecting the economy, workforce, and leadership necessary for success in the twenty-first century?

Technology. More automation of jobs, new communication tools, and continued breakthroughs in technology require "media literacy" to maintain connections with people outside of organizational boundaries. Today's leaders need to leverage media for persuasive communication and regularly engage in some form of virtual collaboration, as well as manage the vast amount of information available to us.

Globalization. The globalization of the economy and increased global competition requires fast adaptation and innovation.

Increase in diversity of workforce. This trend requires today's leaders to be well versed in promoting anti-bias, inclusive and diverse work settings, and cross-cultural competency. Leaders need strong interpersonal skills, such as sense-making, social and emotional intelligence, the ability to connect to others in a deep and direct way, and skills to promote collaboration.

Increase in pace of change, increase in complexity of challenges and solutions. Fast-paced change and increased complexity require adaptation, constant learning, and thinking/analyzing. Leaders now need to look to theories such as systems thinking, strategic learning, and design thinking to guide their skill and competency development. Leaders need novel and adaptive thinking in addition to creativity, critical thinking, perspective taking, and cognitive flexibility.

## Aligning with Internal Forces

There are several drivers for change within the field of ECE, and we discuss some of the most powerful levers for positive change.

### Deep Passion and Desire to Create Conditions for All Children to Reach Their Potential

The ECE field is rapidly evolving right alongside other fields and disciplines. Our workforce is filled with passionate, dedicated, and committed people who love children. People often enter the field because they want to make a difference and have a desire to help children in their communities reach their fullest potential. This is not a new trend, but we believe it is an important one to discuss since it is directly tied to collective leadership.

When the people in the system see themselves as partners, the work is much more successful. When people connect that the changes they are being asked to make are directly related to their higher purpose of supporting young children, a foundation for sustainable change is created. Top-down hierarchical change is often very short term (if effective at all), and as soon as the funding goes away, or the assessor, coach/technical assistant, or administrator leaves, things tend to go back to the way they were before. Sustained and continued quality depends on ECE practitioners at every level working to grow and develop—not to satisfy someone else or check off boxes on a list so they can go back to doing what they did before, but because they are committed to a higher purpose.

Therefore, one of the most important things that can be done is to help directors and teachers see these improvement efforts as a pathway to a shared goal, and that the ultimate shared goal is for children to reach their fullest potential. Susan MacDonald (2016), in her book *Inspiring Early Childhood Leaders*, shares a story in which she helped a director have this insight about having shared goals with those of the quality improvement initiatives in her state that she was a part of. This shift in awareness changed the way the director was able to look at what had previously felt like burdens and obstacles and instead see them as opportunities for assistance toward her own goals and those of the staff and families they served.

Sustained change will only come about by practitioners embracing their own opportunities to develop themselves and contribute to the development of the field, and as you will discover in this book, collective leadership practices can support this development.

## Underutilized and Underdeveloped Potential within the ECE Workforce

The ECE workforce has been constrained by hierarchy and top-down management, resulting in an enormous amount of underutilized and underdeveloped talent and energy that can be unleashed through collective leadership. Another resource that is often left out of the conversation is the families whose children are enrolled in ECE programs, schools, or services. Families want the best for their children and are often underutilized as informants, decision makers, and advocates.

As a field, we need to make the best use of all of the resources we have available to us in order to reach our goal of promoting positive outcomes for all children. We need to continue to advocate for adequate funding and policies that support continued professional development, worthy wages, access to high-quality care and education that meet the needs of families and children, and home visitation programs that support families in promoting the health and development of their children. The ECE field is working toward professionalizing and trying to raise teachers' educational levels, while at the same time struggling with low wages. These two issues are inextricably linked and directly related to underutilized people in the field: we can't raise education requirements—and quality outcomes—without also raising wages. These are not small undertakings, and they require leadership at all levels. Our field desperately needs families, teachers, home visitors, family child care providers, program administrators, policy makers, coalitions, and funders to exhibit effective leadership in order for us to move the needle on our goals together. Collective leadership is about recognizing and utilizing the leadership capacity in everyone to realize the fullest potential of those engaged in an effort. It creates conditions for shared responsibility and promotes continuous learning from all parts of the system. Collective leadership can help us tap into the underutilized resources that exist in our field.

## Movement to Professionalize the Field of ECE

Nationwide, there has been a call to professionalize our field with seminal works written by Stacie Goffin (2013, 2015) on this subject. Goffin calls for the field to step forward and respond to the question of what defines and bounds ECE as a field of practice (Goffin and Washington 2007), including specialized competencies required of those in the profession. In line with our premise, she argues that this field-defining work needs to be done collectively. This change process calls upon the field to make challenging choices. Collective leadership offers an approach for responding to this call. We discuss this emerging movement more fully later in the chapter.

## Benefits of Collective Leadership for ECE

A deep passion resides within the hearts of adults who work with young children, a passion to help children and their families reach their fullest potential. Historic and systematic conditions have limited the ability of adults working with children to develop professionally, advance, and increase their salaries. The potential exists now to align and direct the energy available within both adults in ECE and families with young children with the external efforts of funders, government agencies, and schools to more powerfully pursue the goal of increasing outcomes for children. Our field is at a critical juncture, and we believe that adopting collective leadership is a way to move us into the next era. How can it help? Recall the following benefits of collective leadership discussed in chapter 1:

- better decisions and increased effectiveness
- increased self-direction and motivation
- shared responsibility
- realizing of potential
- increased engagement and investment
- sustainability

As you review these benefits, think about how each might harness and maximize the potential of our field and what might be possible if all parts of the ECE system could experience these benefits. In the following section, we will discuss the forces for change in more detail and how collective leadership in ECE can help address the challenges before us, take advantage of the opportunities facing the field right now, and move together into a new era.

Adoption of collective leadership practices that support learning and adapting will help the ECE field be able to respond to the changing conditions it faces. By using strategies to engage families and ECE professionals as partners, share rather than isolate responsibility, and increase self-direction and motivation, our field will be prepared to adapt to complexity and change, prepare children to develop the increased skill levels necessary for high-paying jobs in the current and future economy, and take advantage of the benefits of diversity of perspectives in informing decisions.

## Current Field-Level Leadership Initiatives and Opportunities That Call for Collective Leadership

The release of the Institute of Medicine and National Research Council's 2015 report *Transforming the Workforce for Children Birth through Age 8: A Unifying Foundation* has focused attention on the need for the field to develop. There are several field-level and national leadership development initiatives and a growing recognition of specific ECE leadership competencies necessary for success in this environment of increasingly rapid change and complexity, including the following:

- focus efforts to professionalize the field;
- the National Association for the Education of Young Children's (NAEYC) Power to the Profession Initiative; and

- the Whole Leadership Framework developed by the McCormick Center for Early Childhood Leadership.

These field-level developments have both used a collective leadership approach and provided an opportunity for collective leadership to be applied.

## A Unifying Foundation

The Institute of Medicine and National Research Council's seminal report *Transforming the Workforce for Children Birth through Age 8: A Unifying Foundation* provides a vision forward for our field and emphasizes that the development and support of the ECE workforce is essential. The report points out that ECE systems are fragmented, ECE professionals are not acknowledged as a unified workforce and work under disparate conditions, and expectations for preparation and credentials have not kept up with what we know about early brain research. The committee authoring the report recognized that to make necessary changes outlined in the report, we will need to

- acknowledge that the changes will require complex systems change;
- include collective perspective, expertise, and action of many stakeholders;
- increase collaboration and inclusion among the many systems and institutions that serve children ages birth through age eight; and
- adopt a collective approach.

We believe the committee's call to action provides our field with an important vision:

> The committee expects that building on a unified foundation, driven by the science of child development and early learning, will introduce a self-perpetuating cycle of excellence, supported by policy makers and a society that recognize the complex and important role of early care and education professionals; the intellectually, physically, and emotionally challenging nature of their work; and the deep, extensive, and ongoing professional learning required for them to be successful. These changes hold promise for helping to retain highly effective practitioners in these professional roles and to bolster the recruitment of a robust and viable pipeline of new professionals. It is through the quality work of these adults that the nation can make it right from the very beginning for all of its children. (Institute of Medicine and National Research Council 2015, 15)

The ideas and strategies presented in this book will assist anyone called to be part of this change in a deepening of collective leadership practice and will support the "collective approach" called for by the committee.

## A Call for Action

As mentioned earlier, author Stacie Goffin is encouraging the ECE field to organize as a profession. In the foreword of Goffin's *Early Childhood Education for a New Era*, Mary Jean Schumann (2013) identifies four lessons from the nursing profession for ECE to guide our efforts toward organizing as a field of practice:

- Identify a unique body of knowledge that is known and practiced by every member of the profession.
- Identify and stay focused on the field's core work.
- Champion field-wide leadership by identifying or creating an over-arching umbrella organization that facilitates inclusive consensus building.
- Prepare every new and existing member of the profession to lead.

Toward this end, Goffin (2013, 56–57) urges us to change together through both individual and field-wide leadership: "Moving forward as a professionally competent field of practice requires not only individual and institutional leadership, but also field-wide leadership—leadership focused on advancing fields of practice to higher levels of capability."

In *Professionalizing Early Childhood Education As a Field of Practice: A Guide to the Next Era*, Goffin (2015) discusses "conversations of intent" as the vehicle for advancing us toward mutual understanding, collective decision making, and purposeful action. She writes, "The systemic change that lies ahead is best achieved through collective leadership and the real-time learning that comes from immersing in a complex change process" (6).

NAEYC's Power to the Profession has begun to do just that. NAEYC created the two-year initiative in response to calls to action to address the fragmentation of the field from both Goffin's work and the Institute of Medicine and National Research Council's 2015 report. The goals of Power to the Profession are to define our professional field of practice and unify our field. From our perspective, this initiative is a perfect example of collective leadership in action. This national collaboration will provide the ECE field the chance to contribute to the development of a framework of professional guidelines, including competencies and qualifications as well as career pathways and compensation. To inform the development of this framework, NAEYC has created a task force comprising fifteen national organizations and more than thirty national stakeholder groups. Early childhood educators, experts, and researchers; families; and other interested individuals can contribute their perspectives through virtual and in-person town hall meetings. These efforts to include all voices at all levels of the ECE system and get feedback on the development of the framework from those who will be affected by it are collective leadership practices.

## Whole Leadership

The McCormick Center for Early Childhood Leadership at National Louis University recently released the framework of Whole Leadership (Abel, Talan, and Masterson 2017). To develop the framework, the McCormick Center used a similar collective leadership approach as NAEYC's Power to the Profession, taking time to gather comments from the field through a series of blog posts and articles and during its 2016 conference. The resulting framework recognizes that early childhood leaders need skills and competencies in three domains: leadership essentials, administrative leadership, and pedagogical leadership. This work is important to the leadership development of our field, as it calls out different leadership domains necessary in ECE. Further, these domains can be at individual, program, or agency level, meaning that not every person who is a program leader would need to be fully proficient in each domain. Instead, there might be multiple people in a program or organization who together possess the skills in the leadership domains. This aligns with the idea that leadership can be a journey among people rather than the skills of one individual.

## Leadership as a Radical Act

Our field needs everyone to challenge old beliefs and mental models about leadership. Many people working in ECE do not see themselves as leaders, nor do they think they ever will be one. Their concept of leadership is someone telling them what to do; they are often directed by other people and don't often have a say in decisions or direction. Many believe that only certain types of people can be leaders and that leadership is some special skill or gift that only a select few possess. Even directors and administrators may see themselves as managers and not leaders. The idea that everyone can have a voice and that all people can develop agency and contribute to and influence positive change is not only new for many—it's a radical act.

## Reaching Our Goals Together: Connections between Collective Leadership and ECE Work

The Institute of Medicine and National Research Council's (2015, 15) call to action sets forth an important goal for our field: that the nation "make it right from the very beginning for all of its children." However, this goal can only be achieved universally under the following conditions:

- We need all early childhood practitioners to view themselves as professionals, which requires a shift in identity that will lead to changes in behavior aligned with continuous learning and providing high-quality care.
- We need alignment in competency development within the different parts of the early childhood system—teachers, directors, coaches, mentors, technical assistance, staff in government agencies, funders, and colleges and universities who are preparing future teachers and leaders. We need effective leadership at every level

of the system and across systems in partnerships with education, health care, libraries, and other organizations that also serve children and families.

- We need all the adults working in ECE to be empowered. A key purpose of education is to empower children through effective and high-quality education. The parallel process in ECE is one that recognizes that adults who work with children will be more effective with children when they themselves are self-directed, high achieving, and working in nurturing environments that support their growth, development, and self-expression.

These conditions can come to life if we reimagine leadership from a traditional to a more collective approach. To help you begin to reimagine your own leadership, we invite you to consider the following:

You can't get to where you want to go by yourself. There isn't anything related to furthering the goals of those in the field who care about the education, growth, and development of young children that can be accomplished by one person. Everyone is operating within a system, and for children to be well served at every age and throughout their early childhood, all the classrooms they are in need to be high quality if they are to learn, retain their growth, and continue to thrive in order to reach their potential. The old quote says it perfectly: if you want to go fast, go alone, but if you want to go far, go together.

All parts of a system need to be connected to one another for the best knowledge and decisions. The best decisions can no longer be made in isolation. The complexity of our work requires multiple perspectives and regular, continuous communication, connection, and collaboration.

We are living and working in a dynamic environment. We will never know all we need to know because things are constantly changing, requiring us to continuously evolve and adapt. It is critical to see yourself as a learner and to create conditions for others to learn as well. Remember: creating conditions for learning means being a "thinking partner" rather than telling people what to do.

Develop the identity of each person working in the field. Every individual is someone who can be a catalyst for change, someone who can effect change and positively influence others. It isn't enough anymore to say, "I'm just a teacher" or "I'm just an assistant"; it is time for all of us in the field to find our voices as leaders.

In collective leadership, your primary role as policy maker, director, administrator, coach, or teacher is to develop the leadership of everyone you work with—you are a leadership developer! Your reimagined leadership is desperately needed. We need the voices of everyone in the field to be heard in programs, organizations, and coalitions around the country. We need collective leadership.

# 3

# Trust, Inequity, Power, and Privilege

What is needed to develop the leadership of groups of people rather than only one "hero" leader? How do we shift from a stance of individualism to collective capacity? The shift requires a mind-set focused on the inherent strengths of people. It requires ways of leading that are grounded in relationship and that cultivate interdependence. To do this, power dynamics must be shifted, and that cannot happen without trust, transparency, and an honest look at how power, privilege, inequity, and trust influence the way groups work together.

## Trust: A Necessary Condition for Collective Leadership

When we were creating the framework for this book, we developed a metaphor that guided our thinking and writing. The metaphor was of a flower growing in soil. Healthy soil is a condition for the development of a healthy flower. In our metaphor, the soil is trust that is required to grow collective leadership. The flower has five petals, and each petal is an element of collective leadership. The flower and soil are a system— they are interdependent. We believe that trust is essential for the development of collective leadership. We talk about building trust in this chapter and the five elements and practices of collective leadership in chapter 4. Like the metaphor, building trust and the beliefs, elements, and practices of collective leadership are interdependent and occur simultaneously. Collective leadership both requires and results in trust.

Trust can be defined as a belief in the reliability, truth, ability, or strength of someone or something. It means having faith in a desired outcome, belief in capability and capacity, and confidence in others. As a field, we know that trust is essential to our work. In fact, our professional Code of Ethical Conduct states that we make a commitment to "recognize that children and adults achieve their full potential in the context of relationships that are based on trust and respect" (NAEYC 2011).

An enormous amount has been written about trust in education and in the workplace. Trust is considered a foundational element of leadership (Covey 2006; Fullan 2013). It is the most important condition when undertaking any type of collaboration, including collective leadership. There isn't any way to have collective leadership without trust.

When trust is present, there is safety, a deep sense of relationship, and space for growth and learning. A fundamental aspect of being human is connectedness—feeling connected is a deeply rooted desire of the human condition. We want to be in relationships, and trust is a crucial nutrient of relationships. In collective leadership, that desire is leveraged to produce networks and systems that exchange ideas, gifts, and talents, and engage in collaboration.

Some describe trust as something to be earned, something that is not a given but that needs to be proven over time through behaviors. Others describe trust as a gift to be given and received or as a choice we make to take a risk, be vulnerable, and trust others. Which is it? In collective leadership, it is a combination of all three. You will need to shape your behaviors so others can trust you. You will need to give your trust to others and not wait until they "earn" it, and you will need to choose to trust the process and accept that there may not immediately be a clear path or a "right" answer.

In leaderful settings, individuals need to trust in their own abilities and capacities to succeed. People also need to trust in each other's strengths and abilities, demonstrate responsibility to the greater good, and come to the table with good intentions. Finally, systems and organizations engaging in collective leadership efforts must be connected by bridges of trust; these bridges in turn create the path for cross-organizational relationships. In collective leadership, partners trust that others are willing to put the goals and process of the group at the forefront. This may require considering a long-term solution over a short-term fix or considering a wider, big-picture perspective over a narrower lens, and the ability to move between all these perspectives to gain a full understanding of the partners, the group process, and even the goals.

# Trust Matters

In her book *Trust Matters: Leadership for Successful Schools*, Megan Tschannen-Moran (2004) provides a framework called the five "facets" of trust:

- benevolence: caring, demonstrating positive regard for others, supporting teachers
- honesty: telling the truth, admitting mistakes, honoring agreements
- openness: willing to listen to others, sharing decision making and power
- reliability: being dependable, showing commitment, coming through in tough times
- competence: setting a good example, setting standards, holding the group accountable, being flexible

Reflect on the following questions, and then consider bringing the five facets of trust and the reflection questions to your team, group, or coalition to begin a dialogue about trust:

Which of the five facets is the most important to me? Which is most important to those around me?

Are there any of the five facets that I demonstrate often and with intentionality? Which do I forget or ignore?

What is something I can do to practice that facet more regularly?

## Trust Comes from the Inside Out

In *Daring Greatly*, Brené Brown (2012) describes a pervasive mind-set in our culture that stands in the way of trust: the "never enough" mind-set. This is the deep fear many of us struggle with that we aren't enough: not thin enough, smart enough, successful enough, powerful enough, perfect enough, and so on. Victoria Castle (2006) in *Trance of Scarcity* also describes a prevailing premise of "not-enoughness." This premise prohibits us from realizing our full potential because it causes us to live in fear and in a state of constriction. What does this look like? You see only deficits, you disengage from others, you live in fear of making mistakes, you pursue perfection, and you live in a state of self- and other-criticism. This, in turn, prohibits you from fully trusting in the capacity of those around you.

Instead, you can approach the world from a mind-set of sufficiency or abundance, meaning that you practice "self-trust." Self-trust means you do the following:

- You believe you are worthy of belonging; you practice generosity and gratitude toward yourself and others.
- You are engaged fully in relationships and life. You accept that life presents challenges, and you embrace your mistakes and imperfections as growth opportunities, as a necessary part of development and life.
- You embrace vulnerability with courage, which enables you to engage in authentic relationships with those around you. You are not afraid of asking for help or making mistakes; you dare to give your trust to others, and you believe that there is enough and that you are enough.

Adopting a mind-set of abundance is one of the collective leadership practices we will discuss further in chapter 4.

# Learn to Relax

Are you feeling tense, anxious, or maybe even fearful about the idea of letting go of directing someone or a group? Do you want to give the other person or the group a chance to explore their thoughts and reflect without your jumping in and telling them what you think, but you feel uncertain about the outcome? If you answered yes, here are a few questions that you can ask yourself or images you can invoke to help you feel more relaxed as you "take the risk" of letting go of control and letting others share and express their thoughts, opinions, and leadership.

Try asking yourself, "How can I be of service to this person (or group)?" "What does this person (or group) want from me right now?" "How can I best support this person (or group)?"

Remember to breathe. It is well known that when we feel fear or stress, our breathing changes and becomes short and shallow. The simple act of breathing can produce a physical cue to your brain to relax and can help anytime you feel that you might need to draw upon your inner strength. Try this brief exercise: Focus on your breath; be aware of air coming in and going out of your mouth or nose. Breathe in for four counts, hold your breath for two seconds, and breathe out for seven seconds.

Think of pleasant images to help shift your thinking from focusing on bad outcomes to the possibility of success. Imagine yourself in your favorite place—the beach, hiking, a hammock . . .

Imagine the meeting is over and everyone is saying it was the best meeting they ever had. Imagine the smiles. Imagine you are writing "trust the process" over and over in your mind's eye (or actually write it).

An important aspect of leadership is tending to your own emotional, spiritual, and physical needs so that you have the resources you need to support others. To practice collective leadership, it is critical that you take time to reflect on how you "show up" to the work. Self-awareness is important here, and your own practice of self-reflection can support self-awareness.

## The Path to Trusting Others

When adopting collective leadership practices and mind-sets, you need to trust yourself to let go of efforts to control and direct others and to trust others so they can do things that might look different from how you would do them. Once you have learned how to be generous and authentic with yourself as described in the section above, you will be better prepared to do the same for others. By giving people the opportunity to examine their roles in a relationship, team, or organization, you offer a chance for the authentic expression of their thoughts and feelings. You offer the safety to make mistakes and not be perfect. People are hungry for acceptance and connection. By accepting people, their gifts and challenges alike, you will allow them to feel more connected. They will feel trusted by you and will be free to take on new challenges and unleash new levels of creativity and performance.

How do you have faith in yourself and others and create a sense of safety for the genuine nature of all to shine through? Consider these ways to create safety and ensure that those around you feel trusted: focus on growth and development, use language that promotes trust and safety, and let go of controlling behaviors.

### Build Trust by Focusing on Growth and Development

In an article about "deliberately developmental organizations," Robert Kegan and Lisa Lahey (2016) describe what they consider to be the single biggest loss of resources in the workplace: people are spending an inordinate amount of time hiding their imperfections, managing what others think of them, covering up their limitations, and playing politics. In fact, Kegan and Lahey describe this as a "second job": people spend so much time and effort leading this double life that it is like having another job. Instead, "deliberately developmental organizations" are intentional about the development of the people within the organization, which leads to the growth and evolution of the organization as a whole. These organizations place value on adult development and growth, and that development and growth are embedded in the workplace. They have figured out ways to integrate coaching into the workplace and have helped people master the art of giving and receiving feedback that promotes growth and development.

Sound familiar? This might be a description of a child care center that uses reflective practice, the relationship between a coach and coachee in a quality rating and improvement system, a community of practice model of professional development, and perhaps even a model for a collective impact effort among several organizations. The idea of development and growth is foundational to early childhood education—we are in the business of facilitating children's growth and development—so it is not too big of a stretch to apply a similar mind-set to adults' growth and development. The practices of collective leadership are within an arm's reach of what we promote in classroom settings!

*Build Trust One Conversation at a Time*
Similarly, assuming positive intent is another practice commonly found in early childhood education. We are well aware of the benefit of phrasing directions for and requests of children in positive language for guiding children's behavior. People who lead collectively can use positive language to convey to adults around them that they assume that others have positive intent. This allows for a sense of safety in the relationship. Positive presuppositions communicate that you believe in the capacity of the other person and can help set the stage for continued engagement and dialogue. Positive presuppositions assume that the person has done the thinking and planning that he or she is capable of and that the person wants to be competent and dependable. Presuming positive assumptions means that you shift from thinking, "They don't care," to "What might they have to contribute to this outcome?" If you approach others from a mind-set that people care and that you have a shared goal, you wonder instead of blame. A focus on positive intent allows you to switch your focus from the person's character to external factors that might be affecting behavior.

The following chart provides a few examples of how language might be different using positive instead of negative presuppositions.

## Examples of Language Using Positive versus Negative Presuppositions

|  | Negative presupposition | Positive presupposition |
|---|---|---|
| Between a coach and a coachee | What would you improve? | What did you learn today that you want to remember in the future? |
| Between a supervisor and an employee | What didn't work? | When you reflect on what you experienced, what comes to mind? |
| Between a leader and a team | It's time to work hard. | How can we be even more resourceful? |
| At a coalition meeting with multiple organizations | How can we find people who care more? | What might have been going on that made it hard for people to engage? |

Using this kind of language will help create a sense of emotional safety in those around you, promote trust, and enable continued learning and reflection.

Trust, while it can take a long time to develop, can be influenced in a single conversation. One of the best resources about this subject is a book called *Conversational Intelligence: How Great Leaders Build Trust and Get Extraordinary Results*. In this book, Judith Glaser (2014) outlines how the brain affects trust and how to help people develop skills in having conversations that build trust, allowing people to feel safe enough to share their thoughts and opinions honestly with others as a result. Glaser writes that when a person perceives that another person cares about him or her, the hormone oxytocin is released in the brain. This hormone supports trust and bonding, which can help navigate conflict. According to Glaser, when you enter each conversation with the intention of listening to connect and to build a relationship, keeping in mind how the architecture of the brain influences trust and using positive and invitational language, you will build trust one conversation at a time.

*Build Trust by Letting Go of Controlling Behaviors*
Healthy relationships involve risk-taking for growth and development to occur. Risk-taking can feel uncertain and uncomfortable for both people—the one who may be stepping back from a more directive

role and the one who is being asked to step forward into a more self-directing or self-expressed role. Here are some things to keep in mind that might be helpful in managing the very normal sense of discomfort when taking risks, letting go of control, and trusting those around you:

- Remember to appreciate the humanness and dignity of the other person. Acknowledge that not only are diverse perspectives and worldviews a normal part of collaboration, but also that they actually contribute to a richer, fuller understanding and will help you achieve better results.
- Recognize that you actually can't be in control. What you can do is create a container for dialogue; hold space for sharing, learning, and inquiry; and support systems of accountability. Even though letting go of a need to dominate or be in control can be a challenge in part because our brains are uncomfortable with uncertainty, releasing the need to control can be liberating.
- Attend to the human need for connection. Make time to share stories about your personal life and your own humanness. In other words, take off your "mask" and show up as yourself.
- Be patient—these approaches take time! Be gentle with yourself and with those around you, while at the same time holding on to the shared vision and goals you have created with one another.

## Last but Not Least: Trust the Process

Parker Palmer (1998), author, educator, and activist, writes,

Whether we know it or not, like it or not, honor it or not, we are embedded in community. Whether we think of ourselves as biological creatures or spiritual beings or both, the truth remains: we were created in and for a complex ecology of relatedness, and without it we wither and die. This simple fact has critical implications: community is not a goal to be achieved but a gift to be received. When we treat community as a product that we must manufacture instead of a gift we have been given, it will elude us eternally. When we try to "make community happen," driven by desire, design, and determination—places within us where the ego often lurks—we can make a good guess at the outcome: we will exhaust ourselves and alienate each other, snapping the connections we yearn for. Too many relationships have been diminished or destroyed by a drive toward "community-building" which evokes a grasping that is the opposite of what we need to do: relax into our created condition and receive the gift we have been given.

This quote can be descriptive of practicing collective leadership. Collective leadership often requires letting go of control and drive and relaxing into a "created condition." This is a helpful way to describe the final aspect of trust related to collective leadership: trust the process. Keep in mind that because collective leadership is about collaboration and collective voice, it is not always clean, clear, or smooth. It can be a slow process and requires patience. Reminding yourself that collective leadership is a process and a journey can be helpful when, inevitably, your team, organization, or coalition hits bumps in the road along the way.

Georgianna Duarte, Adams Endowed Chair and Professor of Early Childhood Education in the Department of Teaching and Learning at Indiana State University, describes her involvement in a year-long collective leadership process:

> I was involved in mentoring global leaders from six countries over a year of Skype meetings and collaboration. We developed a shared vision, identified and built on the strengths of the members, and practiced ongoing reflection and continuous learning. Trust was achieved through conflict, open, authentic ownership, and conversation over a year of continuous contact.

For now, we will share one of our favorite resources to help us remember to trust the process: Angeles Arrien's *The Four-Fold Way*. In this book, she describes four universal archetypes within healthy communities: Visionary, Teacher, Warrior, and Healer. She shares the information with an invitation for balance—for individuals and communities— through the expression of these four archetypes. The Teacher archetype is about letting go of attachments to outcomes. The Way of the Teacher is to be open to the outcome but not attached to the outcome. This guiding principle means that the teacher "has wisdom, teaches trust, and understands the need for detachment" (Arrien 1993, 109). Wisdom grows from trust, and as a result, there is clarity, objectivity, discernment, and detachment. We become open to all options and aware of the unfolding. This requires being comfortable with uncertainty, something many leadership authors remind us to do in this age of complexity. Arrien reminds us that "the opposite of trusting in the unexpected is trying to control the uncontrollable—clearly an impossible task" (111). She defines detachment as "the capacity to care deeply from an objective place. . . .

When we are detached, we are able to calmly observe our reactions to situations and not get pulled into an emotional position" (112).

Collective leadership requires learning and development as a group moves toward shared goals, and this type of leadership is embedded in relationships. Relationships are built upon trust. As the Kellogg Leadership for Community Change (2008, 93) initiative reminds us, "Collective leadership arises when individual leaders come together around a shared goal; developing leaders who are ready to move toward collective leadership is an integral part of this work. Strong individual leadership and strong collective leadership arise, in part, from strong relationships."

Glory Ressler, director of education at Canadian Mothercraft Society, describes how building trust between partners in a coalition leads to promoting a common goal:

> As a result of service providers building trust and collaborating, there was an increase in both knowledge sharing and referrals between agencies. A decision-making process emerged that focused on the best interests of the children and families, rather than on the needs and work of the individual agencies and programs.

Many tools exist that can be used to build trust in groups, teams, or collaborations. We have used the Johari Window, a group activity that provides a venue for sharing information and feedback between group members, and a mapping activity, Mapping the Sectors of Involvement, that can be used in coalitions to help identify roles and relationships of participating organizations. Both tools are available in *Collective Leadership Works: Preparing Youth and Adults for Community Change* (Kellogg Leadership for Community Change 2008), a tool kit with several helpful resources for using collective leadership.

## Reflection Questions

Now that you've read about trust, take a moment to reflect on the following questions and think about your own trust—trust in yourself, trust in others, and trust in process:

How willing am I to allow myself the courage not to have all the answers up front?

What is my comfort in believing that people are inherently good, creative, and competent?

Do I recognize that it is not my role to control but to facilitate others' compassion, competence, and creativity?

What is my reaction to change? To uncertainty?

When I think of a time when I have been able to manage uncertainty, what are some things that helped me to be successful? How can I tap into those resources in the future when I am facing uncertainty?

## Inequity, Power, and Privilege

It's no secret that inequity is a major factor in educational outcomes. In *Squandering America's Future: Why ECE Policy Matters for Equality, Our Economy, and Our Children*, Susan Ochshorn (2015) provides a solid case that educational equity is "elusive" and that disparities are alive and well in our educational system. Although many consider education to be the "great equalizer," access to equal educational opportunities is only the reality for a select few (US Department of Education 2013). Add to this dynamic the fact that many individuals in the ECE workforce face economic insecurity (Whitebook, McLean, and Austin 2016) and that leaders in education have been called to adopt a social justice orientation (DeMatthews 2016), and it becomes clear that inequity and social justice cannot be left out of any discussions about leadership in the ECE field. In fact, social justice and anti-bias leadership are core elements of effective leadership in our profession (Sykes 2014; Derman-Sparks, LeeKeenan, and Nimmo 2014).

The NAEYC (2011) Code of Ethical Conduct provides clear guidelines for our profession related to equity and diversity. The document states that we, as ECE professionals, commit to the following:

- Recognize that children are best understood and supported in the context of family, culture, community, and society.
- Respect the dignity, worth, and uniqueness of each individual (child, family member, and colleague).
- Respect diversity in children, families, and colleagues.
- Recognize that children and adults achieve their full potential in the context of relationships that are based on trust and respect.

These core values are essential to successful collective leadership. Individuals who lead collectively must understand the context that surrounds and influences our colleagues; respect the dignity, worth, and uniqueness of each individual; respect diversity; and promote relationships built on trust and respect. A collective leadership approach is, at its very core, inclusive and is a model for efforts promoting social justice and equity.

## Definitions

Before you explore how power and privilege are affecting you, your team, or organization, we have included a few definitions to set the context.

Social identity. "Social identity is formed when a group of people attempt to see their group differentiated from other groups as a way to preserve and achieve group distinctiveness. This identity is informed by behavior patterns, beliefs, institutions and attitudes held by a particular group. People have several social identities because they tend to belong to two or more groups. Sometimes, a person's identity is obvious (e.g. a woman, a person of color); at other times, an inappropriate identity may be incorrectly imposed on the person" (Lee 2007, 7).

Culture. According to the NAEYC (2011) Code of Ethical Conduct, "the term culture includes ethnicity, racial identity, economic level, family structure, language, and religious and political beliefs."

Power. Power is "the ability or official capacity to exercise authority; control" (*American Heritage Dictionary Online*, accessed 2017a).

Privilege. "A special advantage . . . or benefit granted to or enjoyed by an individual [or] class" (*American Heritage Dictionary Online*, accessed 2017b).

Structural racism. Structural racism "refers to a system of social structures that produces cumulative, durable, race-based inequalities. It is also a method of analysis that is used to examine how historical legacies, individuals, structures, and institutions work interactively to distribute material and symbolic advantages and disadvantages along racial lines" (Leadership Learning Community 2010, 3).

Inequity affects who is in leadership positions, how leadership is exercised and expressed, group dynamics, and how leadership is or isn't shared. Issues such as inequality, diversity, implicit bias, power, and privilege must be actively considered in collective leadership. For example, you may remember a time when there was a dominating person or group of people in a meeting or involved in decision making, and collective intelligence was stifled. Collective intelligence is an important part of collective leadership. Only when all voices are heard from all parts of the system can this intelligence really reflect what is actually needed to move forward most successfully.

Often power and privilege are invisible to people with positional power. People who feel safe to share what they think at all times are often unaware of what it is like for those who don't experience this safety. In organizations there is often a disconnect between the perceptions of what is safe between managers and those they supervise. We often hear administrators stating they believe conversations and meetings are safe, and people share honestly. Yet in these same organizations, we hear from people who are lower in the organizational chart that it isn't safe to share dissenting opinions.

Leadership exists within a context and is dependent on the interactions between the members of the group. Leadership that focuses on individuals doesn't address the complex social contexts that create the social and racial identity of group members. Collective leadership frames leadership as a process in which individuals align and create a shared vision, build relationships through honest and authentic communication, take action, and engage in continual learning as a group. This model, in contrast to a traditional approach to leadership (power "over" versus power "with"), is ripe with potential to engage all participants fully and promote equity.

The concept of intersectionality can be helpful in framing the interplay of identity, culture, and power and privilege. Intersectionality is a concept that considers humans as being shaped by a host of interactions of social constructs, including race/ethnicity, gender, class, sexuality, geography, age, religion, and disability/ability. These interactions occur within existing power structures, institutions, and systems, and shape various forms of privilege and oppression, including structural racism. Intersectionality recognizes that inequity is never the result of single, distinct factors. Similarly, our implicit bias, our unconscious attitudes or stereotypes, affect our own and others' actions and decisions, and is an important aspect of this complicated interplay. Considering power, privilege, implicit bias, and inequity from this perspective can provide a fuller picture of the experiences of the members of your group.

Group dynamics often mirror the dynamics in society at large. People do not come to the table as equals, and there are power dynamics in every organization, with people higher up in the hierarchy having more positional power over others. This is true in organizations and teams: supervisors have power over their employees. Power dynamics also play out in coalitions and collective impact initiatives, as funders are in the mix who have power over grantees, and some organizations may be perceived as having more power than others due to a variety of factors, including the amount of funding that is received by each organization.

## Strategies to Share Power and Restore Equity

When moving from a more traditional leadership structure to collective leadership, the sharing of power is necessary. It is also necessary to identify how privilege is affecting the existing leadership structure. This begins with developing individual and group awareness of these issues and the courage to ask tough questions, such as the following: What power dynamics are at play, and who benefits from them? Whose voices are heard and whose are silent? What do we need to do as a group to begin to address those actions that are creating and supporting inequity in our team, group, or organization?

Having skilled facilitation when addressing inequity and asking people to discuss issues of power and privilege is important. Without skilled facilitation, such discussions can become destructive and counterproductive. Here are a few other strategies that might be helpful when making efforts to create, address, or build equity in your group, team, organization, or coalition:

**Be active.** Pursue equity actively. Take time to build the trust necessary to support courageous conversations about inequity. Take an active role in making issues such as power, privilege, and inequity explicit and spoken.

**Take the time.** Allow time for process and dialogue and for creating a safe space to address inequity.

**Cultivate awareness.** Be aware of your own identity and surface and confront your own privilege. What privileges do you have, and how do they influence the way you view the world?

**Stay accountable.** Keep your group and yourself accountable for addressing inequity, and help your group or team be clear about what equity looks like.

**Provide access to tools and resources.** Remember that addressing inequity is not an easy task, so be sure to proceed with intentionality. Use tools and resources to provide structure for conversations, dialogue, learning, and reflection. Make inequity a conscious part of planning and decision making.

**Engage in systems analysis.** Remember that systems are relational—they respond as a result of interactions among the parts—and that any group, team, or organization is a system. Make time for regular reflection and action based on your analysis of how the parts of your system are interacting and what needs to change to make those interactions more effective, collaborative, and collective.

# Reflect on Inequity, Power, and Privilege

Peggy McIntosh, author of "White Privilege: Unpacking the Invisible Knapsack," encourages us to make a list of the various ways we might experience privilege: sexual orientation, class, employment, religion, gender, gender identity, handedness, language, nation of origin, ethnicity, region, physical ability, our family's language of origin, our family's relationship to money and education, housing and neighborhoods (McIntosh 2010). The reflection questions below, adapted from *The Importance of Culture in Evaluation: A Practical Guide for Evaluators* (Lee 2007), can help you further explore inequity, power, and privilege:

Am I conscious that people are different and have their own ways of thinking and behaving according to their cultures, their past experiences, and interactions with systems of power?

What social identities and groups do I belong to? How does that social identity influence the way I look at the world? What social identities and groups do people who don't know me think I belong to?

Do I intentionally set aside time to learn about differences and similarities with those on my team and for them to learn about each other? To what extent do I prioritize building relationships and trust?

Am I willing to engage in a dialogue about how culture, social identity, and privilege and power affect me personally as well as at work? Am I willing to engage others in similar dialogue?

Do I remember to take into account cultural differences and similarities among those affected by decisions I make, and do I regularly encourage others to do so?

Have I taken time to explore my implicit bias (for example, taking an implicit bias test)?

Trust is fundamental to collective leadership; it is the very foundation on which relationships and interdependence can grow. Trust requires a sense of safety—safety to be yourself, safety to be vulnerable, and safety not to need to know all the answers. Similarly, those around you will need to feel trust for you and from you, trust for each other, and trust in processes. Cultivating trust will require paying attention, surfacing assumptions, and hosting honest and open dialogue and exploration of power and privilege. As you will see in the following chapters, trust and collective leadership go hand in hand.

# 4

# Five Elements of Collective Leadership

Similar to effective early childhood classroom teaching, effective leadership is built upon intentionality. Using collective leadership in your program or setting will require you and your team to reflect on your values, vision and goals, knowledge and skills, and practices and behaviors.

To build on the metaphor we shared at the beginning of chapter 3, we will discuss the five key elements of collective leadership we have identified for the ECE field, which are represented as the five petals of the flower. Each element requires an underlying value or belief and can be created using specific practices.

As we explore each element, we've included collective leadership practices that can be used with each one; however, some practices can be used with more than one element. At the end of the chapter, we suggest different ways to approach working with the elements and practices to begin or continue your journey with collective leadership.

## The Five Elements of Collective Leadership

In reviewing many different articles, books, and other publications related to collective leadership for our work implementing collective leadership and in writing this book, we noticed commonalities and themes among them. Sometimes authors used different language to describe the same things, and sometimes there were more or fewer categories in the shared leadership frameworks they were presenting. We thought it important to identify and name the common themes in the works we reviewed and used. Through this process, we developed this framework for ECE—the five elements of collective leadership.

1. Shared Vision and Reenvisioning: To achieve our fullest potential, we must cocreate the condition we are working together to achieve.
2. Wholeness: When people are connected to mind, body, and spirit, the workplace, organization, and whole system benefit.
3. Collective Wisdom/Intelligence: The whole is greater than the sum of its parts; collective wisdom and intelligence exists that is deeper than individual intelligence; one person cannot hold all of the knowledge.
4. Coaction: Things are better when people are acting together instead of someone imposing on another.
5. Evolution/Emergence: When complexity exists, the processes of emergence, evolution, and adaptability are beneficial, and practices can help focus attention on growth and development.

Perhaps as important as the elements themselves are the underlying values and beliefs that are required to create or embody those elements. We had many long discussions about the common elements that we saw emerging from the works we read and from our experience, about how best to present them and how they could help ECE practitioners explore and adopt collective leadership. We found that trust was so fundamental that it wasn't an element. In fact, we believe it to be so fundamental that collective leadership is impossible without a foundation of trust. This is why we have placed the chapter about trust, inequality, power, and privilege before this chapter about the elements. Building trust among groups of two or more requires navigating inequality, power, and privilege, and it is a necessary condition for collective leadership to grow and develop.

## Element 1. Shared Vision and Reenvisioning

**Belief**
To achieve our fullest potential, we must cocreate the condition we are working together to achieve.

**In action**
Inspire one another toward what we can achieve, reflect on and articulate what we hope the future can be if we are successful, and revisit this over time to refresh the vision or reenvision when things have changed.

Groups that successfully use collective leadership make time to share and describe what they are working together to achieve, not just once when they start, but as they progress on their journey together. Sometimes this is described as creating a vision and goals together. Taking time for this is crucial, as it provides an opportunity for members to contribute their voices to the shared vision and see their own wishes and dreams in those of the group. Shared vision serves as a focal point so all members stay on the path together.

As an added benefit, when people feel that they are part of the process, they tend to feel more responsible for the work or the project and become more engaged. Because they have helped create and/or describe the vision, they will also be internally motivated and responsible for the overall success. Daniel Pink (2009) writes that "purpose" is one of the three elements of motivation (along with mastery and autonomy). The idea that finding purpose in your work and connecting to a cause larger than yourself instills motivation is based on research on intrinsic motivation by Edward Deci in the 1970s.

Developing a vision is often overlooked, ignored, or skipped, especially when working on a project or in a setting where it seems your end goal has already been defined. For example, the goal of a coach and a teacher working together is improvement in teacher-child interactions and sometimes even a specific score on an observation tool. The goal of an organization implementing a program might be to reach a target service number. Although these end goals are preestablished, it is still possible to envision together about what success will look like, how the team might get there together, and why the people working toward the goal feel it is important.

Keeping the shared vision and goals present and alive in the daily work of organizations is critical. Without this reminder, the bigger picture, the *why* of what is being asked of the group, can be forgotten, and opportunities can be missed. Sometimes we assume that if we mentioned a goal in one meeting (perhaps years earlier), people are on board with it and are contributing at their highest capacity. But that assumption does a disservice to both the group and the children and families affected by the work of these professionals. Instead, it is crucial to return to the shared vision and goals on a regular basis, to help people remember what they are committed to and to reconnect with their sense of purpose. People want to contribute at their highest potential; they want to feel inspired and connected to the work they do. Shared vision and reenvisioning helps this happen.

What does shared envisioning and reenvisioning look like? Groups can start by describing the conditions they are trying to create. What is your vision? Sometimes this is a hard question for people to answer. It can be hard because they don't have a clear vision of what a desired future is, and they may be stuck in reacting to what they don't like or want. Other times, people are asking them to join forces to achieve something that they have never seen before. This is why it's so effective to bring people on site visits to see something new to them and see that it is possible, helping them imagine the shared vision. Another way to help people picture a different future is through stories, such as success stories about how people are doing the things they want to do more of and in different ways. Groups are able to envision an aspirational future when they are taken through a series of questions that starts with what is going well now and then moves on to ask them to imagine more of that success. Where are you in your envisioning of a different way of working together?

*Collective Leadership Practice: Identify Shared Goals*
Unfortunately, it is rare for conversations that happen through daily work to evoke the shared vision and purpose that actually does exist. Often people working together will say they aren't on the same page and they want to be on the same page because they see that it would make a difference. The good news is that a simple activity can result in a group "aha" or deep insight when the group realizes they are, in fact, on the same page in terms of the big picture. They may not be in full agreement on the strategies to use or how to get where they want to go, but they do agree on what they want to see and where they want to go.

What are ways to identify shared goals? One of the things we do with groups in the beginning of any work together is an activity called Appreciative Inquiry (appendix B) that asks people to surface their hopes and dreams for the work and the organization. This simple activity can be done in less than an hour and leaves people feeling empowered to proceed together in their work toward a shared goal—after realizing that their colleagues all want the same thing as they do. Sometimes people feel surprised that they share a common motivation and purpose. Gone will be the days of hearing people say that someone doesn't care or isn't interested in the goals of the program or organization because everyone will hear the same dreams and wishes from all those involved.

We have done this activity with schools, ECE programs, board members, coaches, and coalitions. By adopting this and other practices in this book, your group will be intentionally and naturally reminded that you actually have a shared vision, as opposed to something that is preestablished and just written on paper. When people answer the kinds of discovery questions that reveal a shared vision, you will be powerfully reminded that your team cares about children and families and wants to help them thrive and reach their potential.

*The Two-Hat Issue: Shared Vision in Organizations and Coalitions*
Sometimes people in leadership positions in organizations fear that their staff members have individual goals that are not aligned with the organization or system goals. This can also be a potential barrier in coalitions and is sometimes called the "two-hat" issue, where only one "hat" is worn at a time. Members of the coalition are asked to participate as a representative of an organization, and yet they are asked to take their organizational hat off at meetings and put on the coalition hat. This can be challenging to do, and this is why it is critical to have a shared vision for any group, even more so when people from different organizations are part of a group. Behavior matters; group members will watch others to see if they can trust that people are in fact acting for the good of the whole rather than for their own self-interest or the interest of their organization. How can awareness and intentionality of the two hats that individuals wear make collaboration and collective leadership easier? How do you help people on your team, in your group, or whom you are coaching identify and align their individual goals with shared group goals?

Part of the process of creating a shared vision can include a process of allowing people to articulate their individual goals in relationship to the group goals. Alignment often exists between the two goals, and this process can illuminate where they align and where they don't. Individuals often have unique learning goals that can be focused on as they work with the larger group, for example, a goal to learn something or to gain new skills, is a goal not everyone will have. Yet there is no conflict because not everyone needs to have the same learning goals. Intentionality on the part of each person and the group as a whole can assure that individual learning goals are aligned with the group goals.

If there isn't alignment, providing space and time to surface these differences can support future learning and discussion by reminding the members to focus on the shared goals. This way you can be transparent on where there is and isn't agreement, and the group can focus on where there are commonalities.

*Collective Leadership Practice: Adopt a Mind-set of Abundance*
Our mind-set often determines our experience in the world, and it is something that we can both be aware of and take actions to positively influence. Mind-set includes our assumptions and beliefs about the world, other people, the way things work, and even ourselves. The dominant paradigm and mind-set of the professional culture in our field is often one of scarcity, and our field is not alone in this. The larger culture has framed our work in a deficit: we have less than we need, and we are competing with others for scarce resources. The reality is that a scarcity mind-set keeps us from seeing underutilized and potential resources. Instead, Lynne Twist (2006), in her book *The Soul of Money*, encourages readers to switch to a paradigm of sufficiency. By adopting a mind-set of sufficiency or abundance, we literally change what we see as possible and how we might use what we do have to reach our goals. Beth Kanter and Aliza Sherman (2017) have written about the benefits of adopting a mind-set of abundance as individuals, in organizations, and in the sector. In ECE there is often an abundance mind-set when looking at the potential of children. Think of what is possible when we can build these muscles to expand how we think about our colleagues and peers. Sufficiency and abundance mind-sets create the conditions for the higher-level thinking and trust essential for collective leadership.

## Reflection: What Is Your Vision?

Take a moment to pause and think about your team, project, program, or initiative. Has the vision been clearly articulated? If so, can you write it down (or locate where it is in writing)? How does this vision align with your own values or what you hope to accomplish as a professional in the ECE field? Write down a few common goals you have with the vision of your program, team, or initiative.

If your team has not yet articulated a vision, take a moment to think about what you believe is the vision. Next, write down a few ideas that you could use to try to engage in some discussions about the vision. Maybe there is a meeting coming up that you could dedicate to the activity or someone that you need to consult to bring this idea forward. What would your first step be?

## Element 2. Wholeness

**Belief**

When people are connected to mind, body, and spirit, the workplace, organization, and whole system benefit.

**In action**

People connect to all parts of themselves, and this wholeness is expressed in organizations. They are visibly excited about their work and are committed to the higher purpose or vision.

*Wholeness* is descriptive of individuals and workplaces, teams, groups, and organizations. This element describes what is present when people are connected to their souls, purposes, and passions, not just going through the motions when they are at work. Individuals are an interdependent part of a larger whole as a result of their interactions and relationships with others.

Wholeness is one of the three breakthroughs that Laloux identified for the teal organizations. Laloux (2016, 55) writes that "organizations have always been places that encourage people to show up with a narrow 'professional' self. Teal organizations have developed a consistent set of practices that invite us to drop the mask, reclaim our inner wholeness, and bring all of who we are to work."

Similar to this idea, Fuda and Badham (2011) describe a "mask" that leaders sometimes use to conceal perceived inadequacies and flaws and to adopt a certain facade that the person feels is necessary for success. The problem is that this mask can undermine trust. It can also create inner conflict, as people struggle to align what they truly feel and experience with what they show on the outside. Fuda and Badham write that by letting go of the mask, we can create more of a meaningful identity, one that is more congruent with our true inner selves. This can enhance our relationships and even our professional outcomes.

Collective leadership is about wholeness and benefiting from everyone's intelligence, strengths, and talents. Wholeness is also important for individuals to be connected to themselves, all parts of themselves, so that they can fully contribute as a part of a larger group and effort. Kuenkel and Schaefer (2013, 17) remind us to "see people not only as representatives of a group, an institution, a party, but as human beings with all their strengths, shortcomings and desire to make a difference."

Wholeness is critical when thinking about changing organizations and systems. Systems are made of individuals in organizations. For change efforts to be successful, we need to care for the whole person who is part of the organization. Attending to the wholeness of each individual results in increased capacity for engaging the whole system toward shared goals.

### Collective Leadership Practice: Skillfully Navigate Difficult Conversations and Conflict

Laloux's (2014) research found that all twelve teal organizations developed skills to navigate difference of opinion and conflict in their workforce. Difference of opinion is not a bad thing; it's a good thing. We want to avoid groupthink, or seeming agreement that can happen because people are afraid to speak up. Difference of opinion becomes challenging when people take things personally and destructive emotions play out in the relationships in the workplace. The good news is that navigating a difficult conversation is a skill that can be learned. People need to be willing to face issues when they arise rather than avoiding them, which can lead to escalation and blowups. Sheila Olan-MacLean is executive director at Compass Early Learning and Care. This organization is implementing collective leadership and teal practices. Olan-MacLean mentioned this as a critical step in her team's journey:

> *Conflict resolution was an issue that we dealt with by digging deep into learning about it. At first, we had some staff who said we don't have conflict; we just deal with things and we move on. We had to look deeper and see that people were avoiding things that would get buried and then explode. So it wasn't that we didn't have conflict—it was that we weren't bringing up things that were important because we didn't want to rock the boat. That led to explosions. We had to ask ourselves, how can we have those difficult conversations and move to a different understanding of each other?*

When difficult and challenging conversations are held with a focus on the shared goals, with trust and valuing and respecting each person's experience and opinion, success can be achieved. We don't often arrive in the workforce skilled in navigating conflict and difficult conversations, so adults need to specifically build skills in this arena together for collective leadership to be successful. This skill set is necessary for wholeness, rather than suppression or arguments, to exist in the workplace.

Restorative practices build a sense of community, strengthen relationships, and can also address conflict (National Opportunity to Learn Campaign 2014). These practices have been used in many settings, including in schools to promote a healthy school climate. Resources like this can help support you and your team in negotiating conflict.

*Collective Leadership Practice: Practice Self-Care and Build Resiliency*

Early childhood programs and systems are demanding for employees; there are often competing demands from children and families in the programs, the staff working directly with them, and the administrators who are supporting the operations. There are often demands linked to funding and other resources. Self-care is critical at the individual level and at all levels of the organization and the field as a whole.

Wholeness is about paying attention to and caring for all aspects of yourself in the workplace. Our field is full of passionate people who believe deeply in our cause. We also tend to focus on nurturing others. These characteristics can help us be more effective in our work, but they can also prevent us from noticing when we need to refuel. *Burnout* is the term used to describe the condition when people (typically in the helping professions) feel mentally, emotionally, and sometimes physically exhausted from stress or simply working too hard. Practicing self-care with intentionality can help prevent burnout and is arguably one of the most important things you can do for yourself and your team. To take care of others, we must take care of ourselves first. Self-care does not necessarily mean just pampering yourself. It means putting practices into place to support the healthiest life possible: getting enough sleep, waking up early enough to eat breakfast, taking time to eat lunch, getting regular exercise, practicing mindfulness, and engaging in practices and activities that restore your sense of balance.

## Reflection: What Do You Believe about Self-Care?

Take a moment to answer the following questions:

Is self-care something you think is necessary to your professional role, or is it something you consider "extra" and only do if you have time?

Imagine a time when you felt you had all the energy you needed, and you felt invigorated and alive. What things were in place for you at that time? Write them down. Now see if you can pick one thing from that list and brainstorm a few ideas of practices you can put into place tomorrow to rekindle that sense of wholeness for yourself.

Resiliency, your ability to bounce back from setbacks or disappointments, is important for individuals, teams, organizations, and fields. Being intentional about building the resiliency of your team or organization as a whole can be helpful in the process of implementing changes and trying new things. Beth Kanter (2017) suggests several ways to build resiliency. For leaders, a sense of connectedness, kindness, happiness, flexibility, and a belief that life is meaningful are a few. In addition, mind-set shifts (from negative to more positive focused), mindfulness, and simple techniques and practices such as expressions of gratitude can also promote resiliency. How might resiliency support you as you begin to adopt collective leadership with those around you? Celebrating successes, creating safety and a culture of learning so that mistakes are learning experiences, and keeping in mind the higher purpose of the work can all support the change process.

Skilled early childhood educators work with young children to build empathy and compassion in the classroom. Similarly, empathy and compassion can support leadership development in adults. In our earlier chapter about trust, we made the point that for trust to develop, there needs to be a sense of safety, which is supported by a climate of compassion and kindness. We also know that many of us forget to practice self-compassion. In an online article from *Mindful* magazine,

Kristin Neff (2016) describes self-compassion as having three components: being kind to ourselves, remembering that imperfection is a shared human experience, and practicing mindfulness. Self-compassion is presented by Neff as an alternative to the "self-esteem" movement of comparing ourselves to others or feeling special and above average. As she points out, it is impossible for every human being on the planet to be above average at the same time.

Instead, Neff encourages us to feel good about ourselves in a different way: self-compassion. Self-compassion doesn't involve a positive evaluation of ourselves. Instead, it means relating to ourselves in a caring and supportive way and extending the same compassion to ourselves that we extend to others. Being compassionate (and self-compassionate) includes a sense of connectedness as the underlying reason for compassion. Suffering is a shared human experience, and we are all deserving of compassion. Compassion is always there for you. This might be a profound realization for some. But accepting our failures and imperfections and practicing self-compassion is not only a way to be kind and nurturing to ourselves—it is necessary to collective leadership. By practicing self-compassion and encouraging those around you to do the same, you will promote a culture of learning and continue to support the sense of safety and trust it takes to try new things and learn as a group or team.

## Element 3. Collective Wisdom/Intelligence

**Belief**
The whole is greater than the sum of its parts; collective wisdom and intelligence exists that is deeper than individual intelligence; one person cannot hold all of the knowledge.

**In action**
Humility and authentic invitations to share result in deep inquiry that reveals information and wisdom from the whole group or system, which surpasses anything known previously.

Traditional leadership and hierarchies cannot cope with complexity. When there is low complexity, pyramid structures and hierarchy can work well: a few people at the top can make sense of all the factors and can make good decisions. But when complexity is high, the effectiveness of a pyramid or hierarchy breaks down. The few people at the top—no matter how smart they are—can't get enough information or process the amount of information when making decisions to effectively navigate the complexity successfully (Laloux 2016).

When people are interacting with others, there is always the possibility that they can cocreate knowledge that is more expansive and complete than what is available when they are being directed by others, without a chance to share their own knowledge, thoughts, beliefs, and values. When people are directing others, developing strategic plans, or implementing directives from others in their system and ecosystems without input from those being affected by the decisions, opportunity is missed. For example, when you engage the families and community members who are receiving services in the decision-making processes, you unleash a vast amount of perspective and collective wisdom/intelligence. The element of collective wisdom/intelligence invites exploration of the benefits of bringing more voices and ideas into conversations so that wisdom emerges. This collective wisdom/intelligence allows for more thoughtful and effective work in all aspects and is especially visible in the practices of rotating roles and responsibilities and shared decision making.

### Collective Leadership Practice: Rotate and/or Share Roles and Responsibilities

Who does what in a group or organization is often defined by rigid job descriptions and job titles, even more so in school districts or government agencies. Sometimes, by default, people defer to position titles in boards or coalitions, and this practice often leads to underutilization of most members, overdependence on a few, and a lack of sustainability, because when one person leaves, skills, knowledge, and experiences leave too. A group member who is not the highest on the organization chart might be more skilled than the person at the top at something that affects the whole group, such as meeting facilitation. If the person with a particular job title doesn't have skills as high and doesn't yield this role or responsibility, the entire group is negatively affected with ineffective meetings.

Chair/president, vice-chair, secretary, and treasurer are traditional board roles/titles and are sometimes used in coalitions, networks, and collective impact initiatives for "steering committees." These roles may be carried out in top-down hierarchical ways, where the people in the top roles make decisions and then inform others. However, collective leadership works in a different way: for example, some boards rotate the chair role every meeting so a different person is serving as the chair each time or appoint two or three people as cochairs to share the responsibility and take advantage of different skill sets and perspectives.

One reason to rotate roles and responsibilities is that you can distribute the skills across the group so the group isn't dependent on one person. Another reason is that it gives people in the group the chance to grow and develop their skills. People have different strengths, interests, abilities, and desires/aspirations. Helping people grow and develop the skills they are interested in helps them individually and helps the group grow as a whole.

Remember that some skills, such as reflection, can be developed and cultivated in all participants/members. Other skills may not be developed by every person in the group (such as data analysis or facilitation), but it will benefit the group/organization to develop a core group of people with these skills, as they are critical for collective leadership and reaching complex goals.

When organizations decide to share roles—by having codirectors in centers, coteachers in classrooms, and cochairs of boards, networks, and coalitions—clarity is necessary. The key to success is to have clearly defined roles and responsibilities so both the people serving in these roles and those they work with know who is responsible for what.

Jenny Edwards, doctoral faculty member at Fielding Graduate University, explains how sharing the same vision and goals as her colead has led to a successful partnership:

> My colleague and I serve as coleads for a PhD program. When we started working together, we decided that we would only do it if we had fun. That has been our focus for the two and a half years that we have worked together. Neither of us has the need to be right or to be in charge. Our focus is on providing an invitational environment for students and faculty. Our goal is to create a successful program in which all people feel valued and respected.

*Collective Leadership Practice: Use Structures and*
*Processes for Effective and Shared Decision Making*
Shared decision making is essential to collective leadership. Involving the people affected by decisions in the decision making results in better decisions. People also feel more invested in the work and the organization when they feel their voice is listened to and they have a say.

What does shared decision making mean? What do you think of when you hear the term *shared decision making*? Do you think of endless discussions until everyone agrees? This is a common first thought. However, this is not what we mean by shared decision making. Getting 100 percent of people to agree on anything is often impossible. When making shared decisions, unanimous agreement isn't necessarily the goal. What type of shared decision making works best in collective leadership?

Laloux (2016) cites three common misconceptions about decision making. The first is that it has to be top-down, with someone at the top making decisions, or that it is by consensus or majority vote. None of these processes are used by teal organizations. In fact, Laloux believes that consensus dilutes responsibility, which is the opposite of what is desired in collective leadership. Remember, the goal is that everyone is fully powerful, not that everyone is equal.

One of the ways teal organizations make decisions is by using the advice process. Decision making is distributed in these organizations, as employees and teams are self-managing. This means employees don't need to go up the chain of hierarchy for decisions and approvals. The advice process is something that anyone can use, whether you are in a self-managing organization or not. When thinking about a decision, seek advice from (1) people who have expertise on the topic and (2) people who will be significantly affected by the decision. By consulting both of these audiences, you will gain insight to best practices as well as unintended consequences.

*Collective Leadership Practice: Identify and Build on Strengths*
Focusing on a child's strengths is a common practice in high-quality ECE settings, and strengths-based practice is a foundation of good home visiting and parent-education programs. Similarly, focusing on strengths of the adults in teams and organizations that serve young children and their families is also important. Research shows that high employee engagement, success, and strengths development work together and reinforce each other (Asplund and Blacksmith 2011). But many organizations operate under a work culture that focuses attention on an individual's weaknesses and areas of improvement rather than on strengths and areas of growth. According to Tom Rath (2015), author of *StrengthsFinder 2.0*, managers often spend 80 percent of their time during employee performance reviews on employee weaknesses and only 20 percent on their strengths.

When asked what their strengths are, some people don't know or don't have an answer right away. This happens for a variety of reasons.

Some don't recognize their strengths because they find what they do easy and don't realize it isn't easy for everyone. Other times, the work culture has focused someone's attention on their deficits, and they are doing jobs that don't match their strengths.

Everyone has skills and strengths. When these are identified and built on, there is a much higher likelihood of success than when adults are told what they are doing wrong and what they are deficient in. In quality-improvement efforts, even if classrooms and instructors are rated at the lowest score, there are still strengths to build on. And building on these strengths can be the key to increasing quality. If you can be flexible and align job responsibilities to strengths, everyone wins. For example, can you consider revising a job description for the people on your team once they are in the job and using their strengths to align with what their strengths are?

Sharon Morris is the director of library development at the Colorado State Library. She shares how she highlights what peers are doing through identifying and sharing strengths:

> *I notice when people are doing things well, find their stories, and tell them to others. Rather than saying, "I am an expert and you should do what I say," I say, "Oh, this person is doing this really well." I find that people are more motivated by learning of successes of peers rather than listening to an authority figure tell them the "right" way to do something. When I learn of someone's creative project or success, I ask if I can share their story with others. And when I tell them, "I am impressed with what you are doing," it is true acknowledgement. It's important for me to be as specific as possible about their strengths and successes because sometimes people don't realize that what they are doing is unique. As I share these stories of success with their peers, I use it as an opportunity for them to connect with each other. I might say, "I shared what you did with so and so, and they might be calling you." They are not only proud of themselves, they are getting connected to peers—inspiring each other. I call these strengths-based conversations.*

A great resource to start building on strengths is to incorporate asset-based thinking into your work. Developed by Kathryn D. Cramer (2006), asset-based thinking focuses on positive, strengths-based thinking and language rather than traditional deficit-based thinking and language that focuses on barriers. Below is what each can sound like.

Take a moment to read each kind of thinking and reflect on which you use most often. Can you think of any upcoming opportunities to shift to asset-based thinking? How might you help yourself remember to focus on strengths in the upcoming conversation?

**Deficit-based thinking.** Not this again . . . watch out; why didn't you; that won't work; oh no, not that again; I'll never make it; that's just the way it is; it's not good enough; that'll never change.

**Asset-based thinking.** I know how to deal with this; what could work; yes, I can; I can name our strengths; I have what I need to support the change we seek (Cramer and Wasiak 2006).

This and other resources can be found in the appendixes: the Appreciative Inquiry tool and the Questions That Identify and Build on Strengths tool (appendix B) both help groups discover and share strengths; assessments such as StrengthsFinder (which identifies an individual's top five strengths out of thirty-four) and the StandOut assessment can help individuals, teams, and organizations (see resources in appendix A).

## Reflection: How Are You Tapping into the Collective Wisdom/Intelligence in Your Team and Organization?

Take a moment to answer the following questions:

Think about the people you work with—perhaps the families and children served by your learning center or your coworkers or someone you coach. Consider how you and those you work with are engaged to contribute and share your ideas. Does your team and organization have regular opportunities to reflect on what they are passionate about? Do they verbalize their aspirations? Do you have processes for sharing strengths?

## Element 4. Coaction

**Belief**

Things are better when people are acting together instead of someone imposing on another.

**In action**

People have opportunities for meaningful connections with each other to build and maintain relationships so that coaction occurs naturally and is ongoing. People make agreements and design accountability structures and processes that sustain momentum.

What is coaction, and why is it important? One of the main differences between working alone, in silos, where direction comes from above, and working with others is that action is taken together when working collaboratively. Coaction—action taken together—occurs naturally when there is meaningful connection and engagement between and among people in an organization. We believe that coaction is fundamentally different from action that is taken as a result of a directive. Some authors and practitioners have called this element "co-creation," and we considered using this term as well. When people are truly co-creating, they are acting together. Kuenkel and Schaefer (2013, 18) write that "*co-creation* of reality happens all the time—consciously or unconsciously. The term is often referred to when people work innovatively on a jointly agreed deliverable while attending to the quality of relationships through respect, trust and genuine listening." How do you attend to the quality of relationships during coaction? Intentional engagement, skillful facilitation, agreements, and systems of accountability can help a group move from inspired action to sustained coaction.

*Collective Leadership Practice: Use Effective Facilitation and Engagement Strategies That Activate Collective Wisdom/Intelligence* Collective leadership as a whole is characterized by high levels of engagement and connection among members, and this leads to coaction. Effective engagement—intentionally thoughtful and respectful invitations for others to share themselves, their opinions, thoughts, and questions—is essential. Just as important are the facilitation and engagement methods that create structures that lead to success. We will discuss engagement in three ways: first, the way that people are engaged in their work; second, the way that stakeholders and decision makers are involved in a process; and third, the extent to which people feel interested, heard, and included in meetings and group processes.

Engagement, an employee's interest, enthusiasm, and energy at work, is important. Laloux (2016) cites a 2013 Gallup poll that found only 13 percent of employees are engaged at work. In addition, 63 percent are not engaged and 24 percent are actively disengaged. What does this mean for ECE? We believe it means that there is a staggering amount of wasted talent and opportunity in our field. Laloux suggests that lack of engagement can be changed not by fixing the employees but by fixing the workplace.

How do you and your organization engage others in communication and decision making? Is it one way from your program to families, from your director to teachers? Or is it a two-way exchange? Are people sharing what they think? Are there systems in place to get and use information from those who are affected by decisions being considered? This is critical because we can't read minds, and people at the top of organizations are often disconnected from what's happening day to day. Without deliberately structured feedback and communication loops, critical information is absent from planning and decision making.

A deliberately structured feedback loop can include many different ways of getting and communicating information from people involved in a program or initiative, but it must be intentionally put in place. Regular and ongoing communication processes such as meetings, surveys, focus groups, and parent meetings can be put in place for this kind of feedback to happen regularly.

Skilled meeting planning and facilitation is absolutely critical for any group that wants to effectively engage others and adopt or grow collective leadership. Facilitator Lauren Tenney (2016) writes, "Facilitation, or facilitative leadership, is the dynamic and effective ability to move a process along in the most inclusive, focused, energized and alive way possible."

Great meetings don't just happen. They take a lot of work to prepare and facilitate, but this work is well worth the effort and can pay off with meetings that are exciting, where people are engaged, feel that their voices and opinions matter, and leave feeling inspired and energized. These kinds of meetings are absolutely possible, but unfortunately, they are not the kinds of meetings that we usually encounter. To have better meetings, there needs to be intentionally facilitated conversations, done either by someone within the group or by an external facilitator. But without intentional facilitation, the work of the group is hindered, and the group will not reach its potential.

Often in traditional meetings, people are bored, multitasking, or even texting one another about how boring the meeting is. There are many reasons why these meetings are the norm, from adults having a very high tolerance for bad meetings to people not knowing how to make them different or better and falling back on what most of us experience in meetings—simple information sharing, one-way communication, and inequity of voice (the voices of only one or two people are heard). People don't listen, don't retain, and sometimes don't truly understand most of what is shared in these types of meetings. Sometimes the person "in charge" of the meeting doesn't want to make a change because he or she thinks it will be too hard or take too much time. This is where rotating roles and distributing authority can come in. It's then not all up to one person. With time and effort, meetings can be vastly improved, leading to drastically better decision making, higher engagement, and improved retention of information.

The first step in running a more effective meeting is to know what you are trying to accomplish. Are you trying to gather feedback? Make a decision? Brainstorm ideas? Create a product? Next, think about the best way to get it done. A common misconception about meeting facilitation is that everything needs to be done as a whole group. Instead, there are ways to facilitate smaller group conversations and then report to the whole group to help everyone get more perspectives. Again, people are more likely to stay engaged when they feel they have something to contribute, and many people are more likely to contribute in a smaller group conversation than in a large-group setting.

It is best to avoid sharing routine information at a meeting, since this is simply one-way communication. Instead, you can try the gallery walk technique: Write the information on posters and hang them on the wall. Meeting participants then walk around, read the posters, and write their comments on sticky notes. This allows people to think about the information, respond to it, and see how others respond as well. You can do this with material you want people to review and with content people have created in small-group discussions as part of meetings. Thinking through the best way to communicate with different audiences is essential to having effective and engaging meetings. For some meetings, you can have staff facilitate, while others may benefit from using a neutral professional facilitator. Here are some things to keep in mind when planning meetings and group processes:

**Build trust.** Remind group members to set aside judgment and engage in active listening and other respectful communication techniques.

**Connect the meeting to things people care about.** Build on the element of wholeness and work to engage the "whole" self.

**Start meetings meaningfully.** Allow people to have time to connect to each other and build relationships.

Use multiple methods to deliver information when it is necessary to do so. For example, use a gallery walk as explained above. Or provide handouts and let people read them and then discuss their reactions or insights. In short, anything people can read rather than listen to is better for keeping them engaged. Invite group members to take turns trying new facilitation techniques, such as those that access collective intelligence (see appendix A).

*Collective Leadership Practice: Make Agreements and Adopt Structures of Accountability*

One of the critical success factors for any collaboration is having clear agreements and structures of accountability. As discussed in chapter 3, trust is something that is fragile at times, and groups need to pay attention to building trust, maintaining trust, and, if necessary, rebuilding trust. Having agreements is critical to clarity about who is doing what. Accountability is necessary for people to trust that the agreements have meaning.

It is common for facilitators or groups to set agreements or guidelines at the beginning of a meeting, such as to focus on articulating what you want rather than articulating what you don't want. However, if participants begin to voice complaints about what they don't want and no one reminds the group of their agreements, it's not only as if they don't exist, but it's also a signal to the group that they can't trust agreements. This can be particularly difficult when there are power differentials in the group. For example, if a manager or supervisor is not fulfilling agreements, a teacher may not feel safe or comfortable bringing this up in a meeting. Building in accountability structures is key so the burden doesn't fall to individuals to bring things up. One group adopted an accountability structure in their meetings to remind them to stop using acronyms because these were not understood by all the participants. They threw a ball to anyone who used an acronym. The person then had to say what it stood for. Very quickly, the group stopped using acronyms.

## Reflection: Who Are You Working with Collaboratively?

Take a moment to think about the people you work with and how you work together. Answer the following questions:

What are you working on independently, and what are you working on with others?

How does action get planned?

Are there regular opportunities for you and your coworkers to brainstorm how you can work together toward shared goals?

How do you work with families toward shared goals?

Are families on your leadership team?

### Element 5. Evolution/Emergence

**Belief** — When complexity exists, the processes of emergence, evolution, and adaptability are beneficial, and practices can help focus attention on growth and development.

**In action** — Things are both planned and spontaneous; ideas, energy, and learning are ongoing as a result of intentional practices and structures.

The fifth element for collective leadership is evolution/emergence. This is just like it sounds: in collective leadership, there is a constant process of intentional individual and group learning, and the results of that learning lead to improvements, adaptations, and emergence of new ideas, strategies, and approaches. Peter Senge (1990), in *The Fifth Discipline,* refers to "learning organizations," and as is increasingly accepted, learning is critical to creating a desired future.

We often know where we want to go, but we don't know how to get where we want to go. That is true with ECE's shared goal to deliver the best outcomes for all young children. We can discover the path as we go, but only when we are learning.

Learning is a critical skill of leadership because the world has become more complex and interconnected. Networks are forming and driving actions, and technology and the globalization of the world economy are creating conditions that are constantly evolving. Today's world requires that we remain agile and adaptable, and learning is the method to translate our current experiences into our future successes.

The terms *evolution* and *emergence* refer to a concept others have written about related to adapting and learning. Frederic Laloux (2016) describes the process of adapting as "sense and respond" and provides the example of riding a bike. When we ride a bike, we engage all of our senses and are fully present. We continuously take in information and adapt and adjust based on what comes up in each moment. This does not mean we are directionless—we have a destination and a goal— but the specific actions to get us to the destination are adapted in the moment.

### Collective Leadership Practice: Engage in Reflection and Application of Learning

In teams where adaptation and evolution are working well, a few things are in place: safety and trust so that team members can share their learning; processes and rituals for reflection; and a culture that supports both group and individual learning.

What are some key organizational values that will support a learning culture? Stephen Gill (2009), in *Developing a Learning Culture in Nonprofit Organizations*, suggests the following:

- Appreciate risk taking as a vehicle for learning. Recognize that deep learning does not occur without some risk.
- Engage the whole organization in a continual process of inquiry, feedback, reflection, and change.
- Encourage groups and individuals to create, organize, store, retrieve, interpret, and apply information. This information then becomes knowledge about how to change and, ultimately, improve.
- Recognize that wisdom does not rest with one person; rather, it comes from the process of people developing new knowledge together and applying that collective knowledge to problems and needs.

Information exchange is one piece of learning, but true learning requires reflection. And shared learning is necessary for collective leadership. It is not enough if one or a few people learn from the cycles of experimentation; it must be the whole group. Sherri Killins Stewart, director of systems alignment and integration, describes how the Build Initiative she works with makes time for the important work of reflection:

> We create the space for collaboration when working with state teams of health, early learning, and/or family support leaders who work together to meet the needs of children birth to age five. We provide significant time for teams to work together without the pressure of a specific project or outcome. This time allows them to think about big ideas, which require the full investment of the entire group. Supporting this type of collaboration and learning is the heart of all the systems building work we do at Build.

Giada Di Stefano, Francesca Gino, Gary Pisano, and Bradley Staats (2014, 5) define reflection as an "intentional attempt to synthesize, abstract, and articulate the key lessons taught by experience." It is a critical component of learning. You may be planning and doing, but without reflection, nothing helps you make sense of your experience or make adjustments based on what you've learned. Reflection also helps increase people's confidence in achieving a goal by focusing on what occurred and what should be kept in mind as the group goes forward. It is important to continue to reflect both individually and collectively to make progress toward our field's big goals and to make progress by developing collective leadership.

# Reflection: How Is Your Work Evolving?
# What Is Emerging?

Take a moment to think about practices you use for reflection:

What practices do you have individually to reflect on your work, personally?

What practices does your team or organization use to reflect and learn from experience?

What practices do you use with people you coach, lead, or mentor to help reflect on your progress toward your shared goals?

What are you learning?

What is emerging?

What is evolving?

What else could be waiting to happen? What is possible?

*Collective Leadership Practice: Provide and Elicit Feedback That Promotes Growth and Development*

When you hear the word *feedback*, what comes to mind? How often do you get feedback from others? How often do you give it? Integral to collective leadership is knowing that there are different types of feedback and choosing types of feedback that promote growth and development rather than types that do not. Paired with the focus on reflection, self-assessment is a critical component of feedback that promotes growth and development.

To be effective, feedback must be given skillfully. According to Costa and Garmston (2002, 24), "feedback is the energy source of self-renewal. However, feedback will improve practice only when it is given in a skillful way. Research by Carol Sanford has found that value judgments or advice from others reduces the capacity for accurate self-assessment. Feedback that is data-driven, value-free, necessary, and relevant, however, activates self-evaluation, self-analysis, and self-modification." ECE teachers are skilled at giving feedback to children that promotes growth and development, and some of the same ideas can work with adults. You don't need to tell people they are doing something wrong or something you don't like.

One technique in giving feedback is to ask others what they think about their work or about the topic being discussed before you tell them what you think. You may be surprised and relieved to hear that they have the same opinion as you and that you don't need to tell them what is "wrong." If their interpretation is different from research and best practice, you do not have to immediately tell them how you disagree. Instead, you can help them in their self-assessment by looking at research or at an example of what others are doing. Of course, the exception to this rule is if there is an immediate safety issue. In that case, you must take action, and you may need to be directive. Outside of an emergency situation, learning how to increase accuracy in self-assessment and give feedback that promotes growth is critical to collective leadership.

One Head Start organization began annual staff assessments by asking people what they were most proud of in the previous year. After sharing the success, people naturally went on to how they wanted to build on that or what they wanted to change. This practice is closely related to the practice of identifying and building on strengths.

## Diving In Headfirst

There are three ways to dive into adopting the elements and practices of collective leadership. First, you can begin your journey by exploring the elements, if they are calling you. Second, you can start by experimenting with one or more of the practices. Third, you can do both, exploring the elements and practices at the same time. When beginning your exploration, adopting the mind-set of a scientist is a great way to be flexible in your thinking—in other words, approach your efforts with a sense of curiosity and experimentation. Trying something new is often challenging, and unexpected things happen. If you view the beginning of your journey as experiments you are trying, you will probably have more success. We think you will definitely enjoy it more. You could also find a friend or two to explore the journey with you. Some groups have read the same book or article as a starting point for trying new things. The tool in appendix B, Trying Something New (or Different) Made Easier, might also be helpful as you embark on the journey.

## Collective Leadership at a Glance

| Element | Belief | Practices |
| --- | --- | --- |
| 1. Shared Vision and Reenvisioning | To achieve our fullest potential, we must cocreate the condition we are working together to achieve. | • Identify shared goals<br>• Adopt mind-set of abundance |
| 2. Wholeness | When people are connected to mind, body, and spirit, the workplace, organization, and whole system benefit. | • Skillfully navigate difficult conversations and conflict<br>• Practice self-care and build resiliency |
| 3. Collective Wisdom/ Intelligence | The whole is greater than the sum of its parts; collective wisdom and intelligence exists that is deeper than individual intelligence; one person cannot hold all of the knowledge. | • Rotate and/or share roles and responsibilities<br>• Identify and build on strengths<br>• Use structures and processes for effective and shared decision making |
| 4. Coaction | Things are better when people are acting together instead of someone imposing on another. | • Use effective facilitation and engagement strategies that activate collective wisdom/ intelligence<br>• Make agreements and adopt structures of accountability |
| 5. Evolution/ Emergence | When complexity exists, the processes of emergence, evolution, and adaptability are beneficial, and practices can help focus attention on growth and development. | • Provide and elicit feedback that promotes growth and development<br>• Engage in reflection and application of learning |

Foundation—Building Trust • Acknowledging and Addressing Inequality •
Navigating Power and Privilege

# Collective Leadership Applied in ECE

In your role as an early childhood professional, have you ever felt like you were standing before a mountain you had to climb? As it loomed above you, you may have felt like there was no way you could ever get to the top. Perhaps you felt alone, with no one and nothing to help you.

Now imagine that instead of focusing on the mountain, you turned around to find that behind you were people waiting to help, each with unique tools, skills, and knowledge, everything you might need to make it to the top if you all worked together.

This metaphor for practitioners in the early childhood profession—whether you are a policy maker or administrator, program director, coach, mentor, or classroom teacher—invites exploration of those around you. It presents a question: What if the solutions to your dilemmas and to those situations where you feel stuck are living inside the staff, coworkers, and families of the children in your program? What if, by changing your position—or turning around—you will find you have everything you need?

That's what collective leadership is. It is a chance to feel surrounded by support and resourceful people. Instead of having a leadership mind-set that leaves you figuring out everything alone, you are part of a team. For directors, this may mean looking at your staff in a new way; for coaches and mentors, it may mean engaging the professionals you work with to find their strengths rather than deficits; and for teachers, it may mean looking at your coworkers and the families of the children in your classes differently, as potential resources. This mind-set can be (and is) used in community-wide networks and campaigns to guide coaching and professional development, and it can even be used by policy makers to guide decisions and strategy. Collective leadership is grounded in the belief that adults can grow and develop to reach shared aspirations in the face of challenges when provided the chance to contribute their gifts, knowledge, skills, and time for intentional reflection and learning.

## Collective Leadership in Roles of the ECE System

In this chapter, we explore what collective leadership looks like for those involved in all the roles in the early childhood system or ecosystem: those who work directly with children and families; those who support the growth and development of ECE practioners through teacher preparation, coaching, and technical assistance; and those who direct and fund systems and system building efforts. We begin the discussion of each role with a comparison of traditional leadership to a collective leadership approach in that role. A key point to remember is that traditional leadership approaches may still have their place depending on the context and circumstances. The key to collective leadership is intentionality, just as with best practice with young children. Be intentional about how, when, and where you use collective leadership, and you will be more likely to be successful.

We share some stories from colleagues in the field—people just like you—who are already using a collective leadership approach. The metaphor of climbing a mountain at the beginning of this chapter will come to life as you read about people who looked around and saw the people in their programs, organizations, and systems in new ways and saw the new possibilities that emerged as a result of this change in perspective.

Remember: in collective leadership, the concept of leadership shifts from something you do *to* or *for* others to something you do *with* others. And it is a way for people in any position within an organization to contribute to their fullest ability, maximize their strengths, and work toward a vision that they helped create.

### Roles in the ECE System

Before we begin, let's take a moment to think about the many "parts" to the ECE system and the various roles that come together to create the system. The following graphic shows these roles in relationship to the degree of direct contact with children and families. In the center are children and families, who are the core purpose of our work. The roles radiate out from the center, forming a supportive web around children and families. This graphic helps illustrate the importance of all the roles in the field as well as how the decisions (and, we propose, the leadership approach and philosophy) have a ripple effect. This is not a new idea—it is described by many in our field as the "parallel process." We believe it is also important to include funders, policy makers, and governance bodies in our discussion of collective leadership. The collective leadership model can be used at every level of the ECE system, and we believe it is the way to create sustainable collective change as a field.

Relationship of Roles in the ECE System

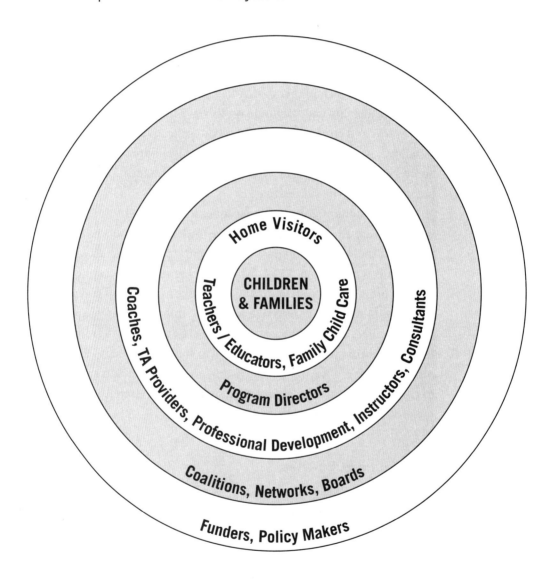

# Families

It is well accepted in the ECE field that families are critical to their children's development and growth. Many programs have made family engagement a priority, although the extent that families are involved varies. Since families are most directly connected to children, it is absolutely critical that they are considered partners in our work. Take a moment to think about your own program, initiative, or role in the ECE system. How are families viewed by your organization or program? Do you provide regular opportunities for the families in your program to provide input not only regarding goals related to their own children but to the program in general? Does your program provide opportunities for families to learn together and from one another?

Following is a comparison of the approach of ECE programs and systems to the role of families in traditional versus collective leadership.

*Families*

| In traditional leadership, families are | In collective leadership, families are |
|---|---|
| • not involved in identifying goals for the child; | • involved in identifying goals for the child; |
| • given one-way communication from the program; | • engaged in two-way communication with the program; |
| • viewed as passive recipients of services; | • viewed as a resource and engaged as partners; |
| • not viewed as having expertise in child development; and | • viewed as experts about their child; and |
| • not involved in program decision making. | • involved in decisions about the program. |

## Collective Leadership at Work: Families

In collective leadership, programs provide regular and ongoing opportunities for families to share their goals, hopes, and dreams for their children and identify ways they can actively participate in making those dreams come to life. Families are included in decision making about the services they receive and have opportunities to share their perspective, expertise, and culture in the classroom or program.

An example of collective leadership applied to family engagement is the model used by Head Start. Created under the Lyndon B. Johnson administration to help alleviate poverty over fifty years ago, Head Start was from the outset a program with family engagement at its core. Families don't simply attend ice cream socials and parent-teacher conferences. Instead, families are part of the governance structure of Head Start programs and guide programmatic decisions right alongside the board of directors. Parents are considered important advocates and leaders, resources, and supports, as well as their children's first teachers.

## Four Lessons for Family Engagement from the Harvard Family Research Project

The Harvard Family Research Project (HFRP) has led the way for family engagement since 1983. Now the Global Family Research Project, this nonprofit supports all families and communities to help children be successful both in and out of school. The Global Family Research Project provides several tools and frameworks to promote family engagement in the home, school, and community settings, and we encourage you to visit its website and explore the many resources and tools it has to offer. According to the group, "one of the biggest challenges in education lies in the disparities—based on race and class—in children's access to the resources and opportunities that promote learning. 'Restoring opportunity' for underserved children requires two-generational solutions" (Harvard Family Research Project 2015). It lists four key lessons learned by family engagement advocates:

1. Create opportunities for parent-generated solutions.
2. Level the playing field by sharing relevant information with families.
3. Use data to move parents to action.
4. Build the capacity of teachers to work with families. (Harvard Family Research Project 2015)

Reflect on how your program engages with families by answering these questions:

What opportunities does your program provide for families to contribute solutions and input regarding your program or services?
How do you regularly share pertinent information with families?
Is information shared in a way that is tailored with their needs in mind?
Do you share data about your program with families?
In what ways do you support teachers to work with families?
How are teachers provided with skills and knowledge to enable them to engage families in an authentic way?

## Teachers / Family Care Providers / Home Visitors

If your role in the ECE system is as a teacher, a family child care provider, or a home visitor, you do the direct work with children and families every day. You constantly make intentional decisions about how to engage and interact with children and families. You might be working with a coach or a mentor as part of a quality-improvement effort. You probably have a manager or supervisor who provides feedback on your performance as an employee and provides leadership and management for your program.

You may discover that collective leadership naturally makes sense to you, and that's because most of these techniques, practices, values, and beliefs are already part of your approach to working with young children and families. For example, you use the element of coaction in your classroom when you establish clear expectations (classroom "rules") for children and use these expectations to help facilitate smooth classroom management. You are already skilled at collective wisdom/intelligence when you identify and build upon young children's strengths and guide children to contribute ideas and solutions when they are negotiating a classroom conflict or deciding the best way to design a marble run.

Below is a comparison of the approach to the role of teachers, family child care providers, and home visitors in traditional versus collective leadership.

### Teachers / Family Child Care Providers

In traditional leadership, teachers / family child care providers are

- directed by those in positions above them on the organizational chart;
- told what their professional development goals are and directed as to what trainings to attend;
- told by others how to improve the quality in their programs; and
- viewed as passive recipients of services, decisions, policies, and changes.

In collective leadership, teachers / family child care providers are

- self-directed;
- able to choose their own professional development goals and which trainings to attend;
- engaged in decision making about how to improve quality; and
- active participants in decision making related to their classroom, program, and organization.

### Home Visitors

In traditional leadership, home visitors

- identify goals for the family;
- engage in one-way communication and assume an expert role; and
- view family as passive recipient of information.

In collective leadership, home visitors

- involve the family in developing goals;
- engage in two-way communication and treat parents as experts in their child's learning; and
- view family as a source of strengths and interests.

## Collective Leadership at Work: Teachers

Tiffany, a second-grade teacher in a large urban school district, tells this story of when she was a new teacher:

> *There was a child in my classroom that had very challenging behavior. He had a hard time following directions and often became angry at the drop of a hat. He would flip his desk over, throw chairs, and yell profanities. I had never dealt with anything like that before, and I needed ideas. We had some team meetings for the child to create a plan to support his behavior, and the team included the child's parent and our school counselor. Together we came up with a plan with a behavior chart and reward system. I also knew I had to create a good relationship with him. I had to make sure he was involved in thinking about ways to help him manage his behavior. I knew that if I wanted his respect, I had to show respect for him. I also thought it was important to make sure that he knew that his opinion mattered. I asked him about what things he liked to do, what things he wanted to learn, and what things about school he enjoyed. I asked him what he wanted the classroom to look like so that he could learn. He liked the computer and to go for walks, so we included those things in his behavior plan. I also asked his mom what things he was interested in so I could include those things in the lesson plans. One example is that he loved to build, so I created a whole lesson on building and construction so he could be more involved. I changed the writing prompts to be around his favorite topic too. It worked—when the lessons were around something he was interested in, he was usually more on task. When he struggled, I asked him to remember a time that he had been successful before, and then I would say, "This is just the same as that other times," and that encouraged him to keep trying. Sometimes the strategies I tried only worked for a while or didn't work at all. Then I knew it was time to go back to the drawing board and try a new idea. I would ask a more seasoned teacher or the counselor for ideas, and sometimes even did research myself.*

Together with the child and the behavior team, Tiffany developed a shared vision (the collective element of shared vision and reenvisioning) when she asked the child what he wanted the classroom to look like so he could learn. She used collective wisdom/intelligence when she built upon his strengths by using the things he was interested in to motivate him. She also engaged in evolution/emergence: she had to do a lot of adjusting to have continued success. Finally, and most important of all, she kept trust at the center. She built a relationship of trust with the child, and she trusted herself to be able to test out new strategies, even if they didn't work the first time. And she trusted the wisdom of those around her and asked for ideas and support when she needed it. Tiffany's collective leadership with the child and the team helped the child have a positive outcome.

## Collective Leadership at Work: Home Visitor

While "home visitor" is sometimes a specific role in many early childhood programs, teachers also perform home visiting functions. Patty Todd, a preschool teacher from Tucson, Arizona, tells this story of conducting a home visit:

*The school was really concerned about the well-being of the child and knew that the family needed some support. The child had issues with attendance and was sometimes showing up to school in need of a bath. The father was primarily taking care of the needs of five children under age seven, and the mother had mental illness. The staff at the school had identified a list of what they wanted to do to "help" the family and were ready to present this list to the father. But I wanted to visit the family first and get their input. I wanted to start with the question, "How can we support you?" instead of the answers, "Here is the list of ideas we came up with for you." When I got there, there was trash everywhere, both inside and outside. I definitely went in with a sensitivity and from a stance of support, and when I saw the house, I realized I had to put aside everything except to say, "This looks overwhelming for you. What do you need?" The mom answered, "I could use some garbage bags." I thought, "Great! Let's get started with cleaning up; that is the logical first step." At that moment, I learned how important it is to really look at things from another person's perspective before making any assumptions about what they might need. I remember working with nurses in our program who would always talk about the deficits, what families weren't doing for their children and what was missing. My goal was different: not to fix but to show up, meet the family wherever they might be at, with whatever the first step might be, and support from there. This particular family taught me to step back, think about my own privilege, pay close attention to trust and to build trust, and to see the humanness in another person, no matter what may be going on. It was a lesson in humility.*

How does our work with families change when we begin with questions rather than answers? Patty set aside the predetermined strategies developed by the school without the family's input and made it a priority to ask the questions first. She saw strengths instead of deficits. She entered the home from a place of supporting the child *with* the family instead of *for* the family or doing things to "fix" the family.

## Program or Center Directors, Managers, Supervisors, and Administrators

As a program or center director, manager, supervisor, or administrator, you are the person who supports the teachers, home visitors, and others who work directly with young children and their families. As the person who is most likely the "leader" according to an organizational chart, you have a unique opportunity to model some of the collective leadership principles we have described. In fact, it is very likely that you're already using some. Have you led your staff in a discussion about the mission and vision for your program? Have you thought about and tried ideas to support the well-being of your staff? Do you ask for opinions from your staff when you need to make a key decision? Regardless of where you are at now, there are always more opportunities to take your application of collective leadership to a deeper level.

Let's use the example of job descriptions and the collective leadership element collective wisdom/intelligence. Maybe you're wondering about how you might rotate roles and responsibilities and increase collective wisdom. Traditional job descriptions and organizational charts include supervisory relationships, and there is often an unequal relationship between the supervisor and those who are "being supervised." However, in collective leadership, this balance is different. In the "power with" approach, the ability of both people to affect each other positively increases. Self-direction and self-management are present in the relationship, and these are balanced with supervisor direction. Additionally, the roles and responsibilities of team members are fluid and flexible based on strengths, opportunities, interest, and energy. For example, during staff meetings, all the members of the team may take turns facilitating the meeting.

Following is a comparison of the approach to the role of program or center directors, managers, supervisors, and administrators in traditional versus collective leadership.

### Directors, Managers, Supervisors, and Administrators

In traditional leadership, directors, managers, supervisors, and administrators

- tell others what to do;
- manage and direct others; and
- make decisions affecting others with little or no input from those who would be affected.

In collective leadership, directors, managers, supervisors, and administrators

- engage others in articulating a shared vision and developing strategies;
- distribute responsibility and leadership throughout the team and organization and promote self-direction in others; and
- include opinions and perspectives from others in decision making.

## Collective Leadership at Work: Supervisor

Toni Lopez Krause, a professional development specialist from Tucson, Arizona, shares this example from being a supervisor of a team of coaches:

*As an early childhood coach supervisor, I was privileged to convene two groups of early childhood coaches at least monthly. These groups allowed me the opportunity to practice collective leadership. My intent was to foster the expression of the expertise and skills of seasoned coaches to support the development of novice coaches. I also hoped to create a climate of shared leadership and trust so even novice coaches would feel confident to express the knowledge and skills that qualified them for the early childhood coach role. These group experiences were an opportunity for coaches to share a coaching story with their peers to explore the factors affecting their work, deepen their understanding of themselves and the people they were supporting, and begin brainstorming ways to approach their work more effectively. At the beginning of each group conversation, I would remind them that the dialogue would be a time not only to practice coaching skills through the use of effective listening and responding, but would also be a time to share and learn new skills from one another. Much of my role was to be a facilitator when the group felt stuck, but mainly my role was to know the individual capacities of the people who made up the group and look for opportunities to facilitate the individual's use of that expertise and skill. I saw myself as a holder of the group's process.*

Did you notice how trust provided the foundation for this story? Toni trusted the expertise and knowledge of the more experienced coaches to guide and support the newer coaches, and she trusted the newer coaches to contribute ideas and learning. She also trusted the process: she designed the meetings to be flexible based on the needs of the group. She talked about taking time to learn about the expertise and skill of each coach and to "facilitate" the use of that expertise and skill. Toni's description of her own understanding of her role as the "holder of the group's process" speaks to the element of coaction: she kept in mind her role as facilitator and intentionally designed the meetings to deepen the engagement of the members of the group. She also was naturally promoting evolution/emergence as the coaches discussed their learning together and reflected on their own practice as coaches.

## Multipliers and Diminishers

If supervising staff is one of your job functions, there are things you can do to work powerfully with individuals on your team and build collective leadership. Liz Wiseman (2010) and Greg McKeown, in their book *Multipliers: How the Best Leaders Make Everyone Smarter*, present their research findings related to what characteristics were common among "Multipliers." Multipliers are people who develop the leadership of those around them. They attract people who are talented and create conditions in the workplace that require people's best thinking and work. They help others define opportunities to stretch to a new level and provide recognition and promote other people's ownership for success. According to Wiseman and McKeown, there are five "disciplines" of a Multiplier: they act as talent magnets, liberators, challengers, debate makers, and investors.

Multipliers are not necessarily "warm and fuzzy," but people do enjoy working for them as they tap into the underutilized skills and talents of those around them. Working for a Multiplier may not be easy, but Wiseman and McKeown say that people who work for Multipliers feel "exhilarated." In contrast, Diminishers create tense environments that stunt people's best thinking. People who work for Diminishers feel fearful—afraid to take risks and thus to make decisions and be creative. The micromanager is an example of a Diminisher. If you are a supervisor, take a moment to think about times when you are a Multiplier. Are there times when you are a Diminisher? Remember, we can't be Multipliers all the time, so try to think about what is happening for you when you are able to be a Multiplier. Maybe you feel your own sense of safety and you are then able to pass that down to your team. Maybe your ability to be a Multiplier is connected to your own levels of stress and self-care. What can you do right now to shift your thinking from that of a Diminisher to a Multiplier?

## Collective Leadership at Work: Center Directors

The staffing structure of a program can support collective leadership. Nora Caruso and Sandy Davie are codirectors of the Santa Cruz Toddler Care Center in California. They shared with us the many benefits of being codirectors. While each has the title of codirector, one focuses primarily on business and administrative issues and the other on program-related issues. They shared that one of the many benefits of this codirectorship is that they are partners, feel well supported, and are able to enjoy the parts of the job they like the most without having to do things they aren't as good at or don't enjoy. As a result of this mutual support, they have been able to stay in their jobs for a long time: one for over ten years, the other for over twenty-five. They have achieved and sustained a high-quality program with very low teacher turnover as a result of the stable and positive environment they are able to create. This is a contrast to many centers where there is only one director. These directors are often set up to fail and experience high turnover and burnout as a result of unrealistic expectations—it is very difficult for one person to do all the work that is expected of a single director. Nora and Sandy say that they have seen other centers with a single director suffer when that person leaves. The result is inconsistent leadership. The board often has to step in to manage operations, and this can lead to an unhealthy dynamic between the board and a new director and can also lead to high turnover of board members. Nora and Sandy emphasized how important leadership continuity is and that they have stability because they work together and provide backup for each other. They pointed out how critical it is to provide consistent leadership of the organization so teachers can feel safe and be emotionally available and present with children. Because of their codirectorship model, they have consistent leadership and can help staff, board, and children thrive.

## Collective Leadership at Work: Administrators

Erin Lyons, CEO of a large nonprofit agency called Child-Parent Centers that provides Head Start and Early Head Start services in southeastern Arizona, reflects on some of the intentional strategies she used to navigate being a new CEO and a time filled with change related to grants and requirements:

> *Going into the job, I was prepared for a personal learning curve, the need to build trust at the organizational level, help others manage the transition, and build relationships in the community. It turned out that there were several unexpected changes that arose in my first two years. We had multiple grant reviews in a two-year period (and the review system was new), we received and began implementing a new grant, and we needed to adapt to the release of the new Head Start Program Performance Standards. Though there has been a clear start to the process, we are not through all of it. We've accomplished many tasks together, and there are still things that are left undone. My goal is to hold the vision of the ideas and intentions that have yet to be accomplished and at the same time ensure that the day-to-day work is attended to. And I still sometimes wish we were farther along!*
>
> *It's important to consider how much information and change people can digest, especially with the pace of the everyday work of our leadership team and the entire agency. There is always so much going on at any given time—we have over five hundred employees and serve over twenty-eight hundred children. It is really important to be intentional about providing context and supporting people with reminders about prior conversations and ideas and making sure that there is*

*documentation of conversations and decisions so that when we meet together, we can be most effective with our use of time.*

*A recent example is when we were planning for two grant applications. I wanted to be sure the process was transparent, that we had buy-in from everyone who would be affected, and that any plans we made included input from as many people as possible. We started with generating a list of questions before we even decided to apply for the grants; we asked what questions did we have related to the grants, what things might we need to consider. We put the questions up in a place where we could receive feedback from many staff members (not just the leadership team). We brought the questions to the leadership team and together established some guiding principles. Then, as we moved forward, we used the guiding principles to make our decisions. We made sure to use historical information so that we didn't forget or leave out something that had been done before. I also wanted to provide sufficient and transparent communication. During every planning meeting, I captured the decisions we made and the questions we had. That way, when we started writing the application, we could return to the notes and the guiding principles—they became a road map to where we were going.*

*Several things made it easier to navigate all the change. First, there were already strong systems in place: the policies and procedures were already established, and overall, roles and responsibilities were clear. I also was able to rely on people who had been here and were knowledgeable about their areas of work and had expertise. Finally, I found someone else with a similar perspective that I could reflect with and use as a sounding board for ideas and reflections.*

Which of the five elements of collective leadership did you notice in Erin's example? In what ways did she use shared vision and reenvisioning during the grant planning process? How did she utilize the collective wisdom/intelligence of the people around her as she moved into her new role? Trust was definitely a foundation in this story—not only did she build trust in those around her by eliciting their ideas and opinions, but she also trusted the expertise of her coworkers. By finding someone who could provide space and time for her own reflection, she used evolution/emergence, engaging in learning through reflection.

## Coaches, Consultants, Mentors, Technical Assistance and Professional Development Providers, and Instructors in Teacher Preparation Programs

Is your role in the ECE system that of a mentor, coach, or technical assistance provider? Perhaps you are an instructor in an institution of higher education. What does collective leadership look like in your role? Do you take time to assess the needs, interests, and knowledge of your audience before designing a learning session? How do you think about those whom you are teaching? Do you consider yourself an expert with special knowledge to share with those in the audience? Or do you consider yourself a colearner, someone who brings information for the group to process, make sense of, and think of ways to apply it to their own practice?

If you build upon the knowledge of the people in your learning sessions, use delivery methods that are based on adult learning principles, and provide ample opportunities for the people in the group to share their own experiences and ideas, you are already using collective leadership. Every time you adjust your planned agenda based on the response from your audience or choose to implement learning opportunities that are based on the needs and interests of those you are "teaching," you are using collective leadership.

If you are a coach and you recognize the strengths of the people you are coaching, encourage their insights through reflection and intentional questions that guide their thinking, and invite them to select their own goals for coaching, you are using collective leadership.

Following are comparisons of the approach to the role of coaches, consultants, mentors, technical assistance providers, professional development providers, and higher education instructors in traditional versus collective leadership:

*Coaches, Consultants, Mentors, and Technical Assistance Providers*

In traditional leadership, coaches, consultants, mentors, and technical assistance providers

- believe they are experts and do not recognize the expertise of those they are supporting;
- drive quality improvement; and
- develop solutions for others.

In collective leadership, coaches, consultants, mentors, and technical assistance providers

- recognize expertise and knowledge of teachers and directors;
- engage others in the development of goals and quality-improvement plans; and
- partner with teachers and directors to identify shared goals and solutions.

*Professional Development Providers and Higher Education Instructors*

In traditional leadership, professional development providers and higher education instructors

- decide what topics/trainings others receive;
- conduct trainings that are informational and transactional—designed as if participants are empty vessels to be filled;
- use one-way communication —expert to nonexpert;
- design and deliver one-time trainings rather than designing and delivering multiple learning opportunities that embed reflection and practice; and
- design programs of study and curricula based on decisions from those within the institution with little or no input from current or potential students.

In collective leadership, professional development providers and higher education instructors

- involve participants in deciding what topics/trainings they receive;
- conduct trainings / professional development opportunities in which learning is transformational, not just transactional—going beyond information delivery and using interactive delivery of information instead of relying on lecture;
- use two-way communication, recognizing participants have expertise, resources, and ideas;
- design and deliver multiple learning sessions, rather than one-time workshops, embedded with rich opportunities for reflection, shared meaning making, and aligned with how adults learn best (not lecture); and

- design programs of study and curricula with needs of current and potential students in mind, with regular opportunities for those groups to provide feedback and input on decisions and design.

## Collective Leadership at Work: Professional Development

Petrea Hicks, an ECE professional development trainer and consultant from Maryland, tells a story of when she presented at a conference on a topic related to implicit bias:

*The title was "The Importance of Fostering a Positive Self Image in Young African American Males through Literature and Imagery," and I wanted to provide participants with an opportunity to share and receive information about ways to surface and address implicit bias, with the overall goal to reduce suspensions and expulsions. I knew the topic had the potential to cause discomfort or cognitive dissonance for participants. I knew it could either go very well or terribly wrong. I had to create an atmosphere of trust from the very beginning by providing a chance to connect. We started with everyone sharing something positive about themselves, and then I made a connection about those characteristics to children. I reminded the group that we are all in this for one reason: children. I shared a poster of famous people when they were children, and we had a discussion about the fact that you never know who might be in your classroom. I shared some of the main points of the content, and one of the participants posed a provocative question, to which another woman in the group responded. At this point, the workshop took on a life of its own. The exchange of ideas between the people in the audience opened up an honest conversation. It was so respectful—just people engaging in a conversation. Everybody was learning from everybody else. I could not have planned it better! Afterwards, people approached me to thank me for the experience and the importance of the topic. It really was an example of a favorite quote from Nelson Mandela: 'Lead from the back and let others believe they are in the front.' After the workshop, I read the evaluations and, based on feedback from a person that said she*

*wasn't sure how she could use the information, decided that next time,*
*I want to pause in the middle to have people think about how they are*
*going to apply the information to their work.*

Petrea used several elements of collective leadership in her role as a presenter and professional development provider. She started with a climate of trust, curiosity, and openness by providing time for initial relationship building and encouraging people in the group to think about childhood. When she reminded the audience of their shared goal—the best outcomes for children—she was using the element of shared vision and reenvision. By allowing the audience to guide the conversation and share their own stories, solutions, and ideas, she was using the element of collective wisdom/intelligence and practicing effective facilitation strategies that activated it. Finally, she used evolution/emergence as she reviewed the evaluations to identify how she could continue to adapt her techniques and continue to improve.

## Helping

As we discussed in chapter 2, efforts are under way nationally to help those working directly with children and families improve their practice and increase quality. Successful change efforts, those that result in sustainable changes in quality, are usually characterized by a strong relationship between those being "helped" and those seeking to "help." We use the word *helper* here to mean coach, mentor, or technical assistant, or to describe someone whose job or role is to "help" other early childhood practitioners improve their practice but who is not the supervisor or manager of that person. Often the helper isn't employed by the same organization as the person being helped (as in the case of quality rating improvement systems).

Sometimes there is an assumption that people who know pedagogical content are automatically qualified to coach. It is important to note that this is not necessarily true. The ability to help another person (adult) grow and develop is at the core of coaching. This is a different skill set than being fluent with the early childhood research. It's not always easy for ECE helpers to learn new skills required for helping, and it can be very challenging to their own identity. Sometimes helpers feel their value is connected to being the expert and telling others what to do. But willingness to share power in the interaction and relationship is what makes collective leadership different from traditional approaches to managing, supervising, and helping.

Edgar Schein, in his books *Helping: How to Offer, Give, and Receive Help* (2011) and *Humble Inquiry: The Gentle Art of Asking Instead of Telling* (2013), writes about this dynamic of helping. In our opinion, what he writes about is an application of a collective leadership approach. Schein encourages those who are helpers to embody humility. Helpers, according to Schein, should create conditions where helping is offered and received in an effective way. Often the person being helped is not actually the initiator of the helping relationship. This already starts the relationship off on an uneven foot, with someone being assigned to get "help," to which a natural response is resisting and defending. This can be positively affected by adopting a position of humility and seeking to draw out from the person where there might be a shared goal, alignment with their current values and vision, and support being offered by the helper. Schein (2011, 147–57) offers the following principles and tips for effective helping:

- Principle 1: Effective Help Occurs When Both Giver and Receiver Are Ready
- Principle 2: Effective Help Occurs When the Helping Relationship Is Perceived to Be Equitable
- Principle 3: Effective Help Occurs When the Helper Is in the Proper Helping Role
- Principle 4: Everything You Say or Do Is an Intervention That Determines the Future of the Relationship
- Principle 5: Effective Helping Starts with Pure Inquiry
- Principle 6: It Is the Client Who Owns the Situation
- Principle 7: You Never Have All the Answers

## Collective Leadership at Work: Coaches

Gaye Lynn Fisher, a coach supervisor, has an example of how collective leadership helped family care providers not only improve quality but also do it as a result of their own empowerment:

*One of the groups we have been coaching for the last eight years that has seen some of the greatest and sustainable changes is the family child care providers. At the beginning, one of the things we noticed about this group was a tendency to depend entirely on the coach to tell them what to do. Here's an example: One of the providers presented her coach with a seven-page list of scenarios and asked the coach to tell her how she would handle each situation should it arise. Because the coach had gone through professional development that helped her develop self-direction in others, she knew that if she did not help the provider learn to think for herself, it would just establish a never-ending cycle of the provider creating the "what if" list and the coach giving her the answer. So instead of responding to the questions posed, the coach asked the provider where she might find the answers herself. The coach got out all the assessment tools and other resources and over time taught this provider how to do the research and find the information for herself. The coach reported this was the moment the shift in their relationship happened. The provider became more confident in her own practice and began to keep all of her tools close at hand (heavily highlighted with notes in the margins). The coach became a source of new resources and help for the provider to think through her questions and concerns. This provider achieved a five-star rating (the highest rating possible) and has been able to maintain that for four years, indicating that there has been a true shift in her practice and that what she is doing now is sustainable.*

*An interesting part of this is it also marked the change of the coach's practice. She called this her aha moment, when she realized this was how she needed to coach all of her sites. From my point of view, this has been a remarkable change, especially for the family child care providers. These women often did not speak for themselves and were not encouraged to by most of the previous systems they were part of. Most are monolingual Spanish speakers and so were left out of many training opportunities and other community meetings that were presented in English. They had no voice and felt that they weren't taken seriously. Now they attend and speak out at public meetings, including meetings where funding decisions that affect them are made. They continue to attend the network meetings and trainings, and many of them know the assessment tools as well as or better than the coaches.*

What elements of collective leadership did you notice at play in this story? How did the coach work to build the capacity of the provider to gain the skills to research and find her own answers instead of relying on an "expert" to tell her what to do? How do you think this affected the provider's self-direction and internal motivation? In what ways did the coach trust the provider's skill and ability? How did the coach's approach support a deepening of trust between the provider and the coach?

## Governance / Boards of Directors, Networks, Coalitions, and System Building or Collective Impact Initiatives

As we discussed in chapter 1, efforts to work across systems to address complex community problems and realize a shared vision for healthy communities is on the rise. If you are a part of a network, coalition, or system building effort, or if you serve on a board of directors, your input, decisions, and feedback affect services for young children and their families. What opportunities does your group have to use the five elements of collective leadership? How can you deepen your levels of engagement, collaboration, connection, and colearning?

## The Engagement Governance Framework

For corporate child care programs and centers, corporate boards are often involved in making decisions for the company that affect many things in the classroom, from curricula to furniture and how the classroom environment needs to be designed. For family home care providers, the owners serve as the legal decision-making body.

In school districts, superintendents and boards of education are responsible for the operations of the schools in the district. And for nonprofits, boards of directors are legally responsible for governance of the organization.

A resource to help boards share power is the Engagement Governance Framework (Freiwirth 2007). This framework was proposed to build structures and processes of community engagement into the work of boards. The framework outlines the governance functions of a board (planning, advocacy, evaluation, and fiduciary care activities) as distinct from the structure of a board. It suggests that a nonprofit organization will better meet its mission and better serve clients and communities by including people from other parts of the system (other stakeholders) in the information gathering and decision making involved in governance—in other words, by taking a collective leadership approach.

Following is a comparison of the approach to the role of governing boards and boards of directors in traditional versus collective leadership:

*Governance / Boards of Directors*

In traditional leadership, boards of directors

- are homogeneous, lack diversity, and do not include representation from community members and those served by the organization;
- use rigid roles and responsibilities; and
- do not practice shared decision making and lack engagement with staff/community served.

In collective leadership, boards of directors

- are diverse and include representatives from the community/population served;
- rotate roles and responsibilities; and
- share decision making with staff, clients, and community members.

Below is a comparison of how member organizations of networks, coalitions, and collective impact initiatives work together in traditional leadership compared to collective leadership:

*Networks, Coalitions, and Collective Impact Initiatives*

In traditional leadership, networks, coalitions, and collective impact initiatives

- are designed to be top-down, with those at the top of the organizational chart making decisions;
- have a lead agency that selects and assigns roles to partner agencies;
- are staff driven and have static roles and responsibilities;
- spend little to no time on reflection or getting input from members and the community;
- use one-way communication to partners and stakeholders; and
- do not include community members and those served by the organizations.

In collective leadership, networks, coalitions, and collective impact initiatives

- are designed to be inclusive and have a diverse membership, interested people, and organizations;
- come together to decide together what the partnership will look like;
- have a diverse leadership team that engages stakeholders to make important decisions about strategy and roles—what they will do, how, and with whom—collectively, and rotate roles to build capacity and sustainability;
- use ongoing reflection as part of the work—work evolves and responds to changing conditions, energy of the group, and applied learning;
- engage in two-way communication; and
- engage partners, stakeholders, and community members, and give respect before it is "earned."

## Collective Leadership at Work: Coalitions

Debbie Curley is a member of the steering committee of a county coalition that was formed with a collective leadership model:

> *Our coalition, Birth to Five Partners, was born out of a conversation among representatives from four agencies that served families with children birth to age five in Santa Cruz County, Arizona, who lamented the lack of coordination of services. We all said, "We don't want another meeting where all we do is put events in our calendars." We wanted a meeting that genuinely inspired collaboration, where we understood what each agency had to offer, and where we could work together to ensure that every family in the county knew how to access the services they needed. There are three aspects of Birth to Five Partners meetings that made this coalition successful, and they are related to our ability to (1) ensure sustainability, (2) set realistic goals, and (3) avoid territorialism. What makes us unique is that the group's direction is driven purely by its members and the community's needs.*
>
> *Birth to Five Partners is sustainable because we have a steering committee that facilitates all the logistics with very little expense of time or money. In addition, members are motivated to attend meetings by a common self-driven agenda. This agenda is set by regularly soliciting feedback from members on the direction the group should take. The group also benefits from the facilitation of an outside consultant who provides a host of strategies to keep members engaged and lead the group to productive results.*
>
> *A good sense of scale helps Birth to Five Partners set realistic goals. The steering committee efficiently delegates manageable tasks and never takes on more than it can handle. In addition, having an outside facilitator also cuts down on time spent preparing for meetings. By keeping the expenses of time and money low, members do not have to make deep sacrifices to attend meetings. Rather, participants usually leave meetings feeling reenergized.*
>
> *Coalition building requires groups to subjugate their missions to the larger goals of the group. Having a neutral facilitator helps reduce skepticism that one person or agency is driving the agenda. This facilitation is key to building trust among members and has afforded steering committee members a certain detachment which helps us*

*be effective as a group. Our funding does not involve programmatic obligations and allows the group to develop organically according to the needs of families and interests of partner agencies. Birth to Five Partners is a self-governing organization where group members have ownership and every member is valued.*

If you lead or are a member of a network, coalition, or collective impact initiative, we invite you to consider what things might be common between your group and Debbie's example above. What are some ways you can promote the group's self-governance? How might you increase ways that group members have ownership and feel valued? Are there any resources you might need to help you be successful? (For example, do you have a neutral facilitator?)

## Funders

While you may have been involved in efforts where foundations and other funders collaborate with each other to jointly fund work, or where foundations fund family and community engagement, the details and requirements of most funding is still dictated by funders. What if funders worked collaboratively with community benefit organizations to create processes that allowed the applicants to choose their goals, partners, and strategies? What if every funding opportunity included community input around goals to be addressed and strategies to be used? How might efforts to "improve communities" look different if they operated under a collective leadership model? Many of these issues and questions apply to policy makers as well as funders.

Following is a comparison of the approach to the role of funders in traditional versus collective leadership:

*Funders*

In traditional leadership, funders

- release requests for proposals without input from community;
- prescribe the activities and strategies they want to fund, often asking for system-level changes while funding individual organizations;
- dictate required partners when funding partnerships;
- offer funding that is restricted, limited, and doesn't allow for best use of the knowledge of the applicants/grantees;
- may ask for grantees to conduct community engagement to develop plans but often require up-front linear plans and goals, which make it difficult for the engagement to be meaningful; and
- allow few, if any, opportunities for shared learning.

In collective leadership, funders

- engage the community in identifying priority areas for funding and share decision making about foundation investments;
- allow the applicants to make decisions about strategy and funding multiorganizational proposals;
- allow applicants to select partners;
- adequately fund infrastructure, allow for flexibility, and allow key decisions about strategy to be determined by applicants/grantees;
- allow time for decisions to be made about the work (identified goals, strategies, outcomes) so meaningful engagement and strategic learning can happen once the grant is awarded; and
- are transparent and participate in reflection and shared learning.

## Collective Leadership at Work: Funders

Cassandra shares an example of what happens when funders both use and support collective leadership as part of collaboration and collective impact initiatives:

> *The Community Foundation for Southern Arizona (CFSA) began a collaborative funding initiative in 2010. I helped them change their investment strategy from one of funding individual organizations*

to one of funding multiorganization collaborations. We began using the Build Initiative System Change Framework. When the collective impact article came out in 2011 [see "Collective Impact and Systems Building" in chapter 1], it aligned with what CFSA had been doing, and so we drew from the framework as well.

People have long been working together from different organizations toward shared community goals. When a goal cannot be achieved by one organization on its own, it can often be achieved when working with other organizations. The 2011 collective impact article outlined conditions necessary for success in successful multiorganization initiatives, including neutral facilitation, coordination, and shared measurement, and provided a guide for our design. These were the core functions that CFSA used to support the multiorganization collaborations they funded, and which were named "backbone" support in the collective impact articles.

CFSA provided support in addition to funding to the collaborations who were working together toward a shared goal that was identified by the groups themselves. Critical to shared leadership among the grantees and the funder was that the funder (CFSA) did not impose the goals, the strategies, and the partners onto the collaborations, which funders often do. In addition, the technical assistance provided by foundation staff and consultants was designed to help the organizations develop collective leadership in their work.

I had previously worked with multiple collaboration initiatives in which the funder imposed the goal and strategies and required certain organizations to be part of the project. This was frequently unsuccessful. A handful of people in each organization said yes to apply for the grant, but frequently, once it was awarded, it was assigned to others who had not been involved in the process, did not really want to work on it at all, and received little to no support from those who had made the agreement to accept the funding. When organizations come together for the purpose of sharing money and splitting up a pot of grant funding, it rarely leads to a successful collaboration. What was different in the successful collaborations with a collective leadership approach was that people weren't coming to the table for money. Instead, the foundation funding frequently went toward the coordination and evaluation, with the staff time devoted from the partners being essentially "volunteered" to support the goal.

# Conclusion

As a field we have ambitious goals for the children and families in our communities, and we are poised to take our unique skills and knowledge about how to engage children in their own learning to develop to their fullest potential and apply them to families, ECE practitioners, helpers, boards, networks, coalitions, funders, and policy makers. We are poised in a moment in time where we have the opportunity to fully align our resources, skills, and knowledge toward the shared goals of the field. Each of us can examine our daily practices no matter what our role in the ECE system and do more to promote the growth and development of those around us. We can help grow our own practice in collaboration, partnering, and working with others in ways that not only empower them but empower us as well. If we are taking on too much responsibility, we can be empowered by distributing that to others. The opportunity is before us to truly change the trajectory of our progress toward ECE field goals by adopting collective leadership. This sentiment is articulated on the Harvard University Center on the Developing Child website (accessed 2017) about distributed leadership:

> Leadership for this movement is bigger than any one person or institution. Its success depends on the shared vision and work of individuals, organizations, and systems. When leaders align their agendas, networks, and resources in support of a shared goal, they have the power to make lasting, significant improvements in the lives of children and families.

In order to achieve significant change for children facing adversity, the field needs innovative leadership.

# Beginning Your Journey: Adopting Collective Leadership

At this point in the book, we've covered a lot of ground. We've introduced collective leadership and talked about why we think it's important for ECE and what the benefits are to adopting it intentionally. We've talked about trust as the foundation and discussed five elements and beliefs essential to collective leadership. We have shared collective leadership practices and what it looks like in different roles within the ECE system. Now we are going to share some thoughts and resources to support your journey in either adopting collective leadership or growing the ways in which you already apply it.

People are using collective leadership throughout our field. We know this: we hear it when we present at conferences, we see examples in descriptions of national initiatives, and other authors writing about leadership refer to many similar ideas. When we asked people for examples of collective leadership in ECE for this book, people shared stories from all over the United States and Canada. Our intent for creating a framework of collective leadership was to bring the resources and ideas from some of our favorite authors and thinkers together in one place. We wanted to provide names to the elements and practices, show how they all connect to each other, and give readers a starting point to think about collective leadership in ECE in an intentional way. We hope this book will be helpful to you regardless of whether you already use collective leadership every day or if you are completely new to this way of thinking.

One of the benefits of adopting collective leadership as an explicit goal is that it will help you be even more intentional about it. You may be thinking about collective leadership in one of the roles you play and can expand your use of the concepts into other roles or situations. You might be using some practices and see a benefit to adding additional ones. Building on your existing knowledge and success makes it easier.

One thing that makes adopting collective leadership different from other approaches to leadership is that you are by definition doing it with at least one other person, sometimes many more. One thing people always ask is "How can we get there? How can we get from where we are now to collective leadership?"

## Change Can Be Harder Than You Think

Making a change is often more difficult than you might think, especially when you are working with others to do so. Adopting collective leadership, whether you are starting something new or building on existing practices, will probably require making changes to the way things are being done. We felt it would be helpful to share some information about why it's often harder to make change than we expect and some resources to help make it easier.

### We Forget to Align Our Elephant and Rider

One of our favorite books about change is *Switch: How to Change Things When Change Is Hard* by Chip and Dan Heath. They are brilliant at taking complex and complicated research and making it simple to understand. We use several concepts from *Switch* regularly with groups. The Heaths borrow the metaphor of a rider, an elephant, and a path from *The Happiness Hypothesis* by Jonathan Haidt. The rider is the rational mind, and the elephant is the subconscious emotional side. Though the rider may seem to be the leader holding the reins and deciding to change, the elephant is the real powerhouse. This means that when making a change, we need to convince both our rational side *and* our emotional side. If the rational mind wants something and the emotional side is not aligned, the rational mind can't be successful. The path toward the goal of the change can either help the elephant and rider (if the change is specific and clear) or hinder them (if the change is vague). So to make a change successful, you align the rider and the elephant and "clear" the path. In the words of the Heath (2011, 24) brothers, "You need to direct the rider, motivate the elephant, and shape the path." This concept is helpful when thinking about the conditions that facilitate change. When you attend to all three, your change efforts can be much more successful.

## We Forget There Are Stages of Change and Differences in Readiness to Change

Many programs that offer coaching to educators do not assess participants' readiness to change before they are selected and enrolled. The result is often a big disconnect between what stage the funders, administrators, and coaches assume participants are in related to quality changes and the stage of change the educators are actually in. Such programs need to assess where the people they are working with are in their readiness for change and rethink their approaches for helping them make those changes.

A useful resource is the Stages of Change model, initially developed by James Prochaska and Carlos DiClemente (1983). The Stages of Change model recognizes that there is a big difference in approach when trying to make a change if the person making the change (yourself included) has decided there is a benefit to changing, has identified a motivation or reason to change, understands what will be useful to help them change, and is ready to take action. This readiness for change is much different than that of someone who has not even considered that there may be a benefit to changing behavior.

We have found it incredibly helpful for those in coaching roles and those being coached to think about the stages of change when implementing change and to be intentional about matching the strategies or activities used with the stage the person might be in. While a center, program, director, or teacher might be enrolled in a program that includes coaching or technical assistance, it doesn't mean everyone is ready for change or committed to change. Introducing this framework helps people self-assess how they feel about change and informs those working with them about what types of approaches will be a good match. If adopting collective leadership will involve a change in yourself or in others around you, it might be helpful to consider the stages of change.

The Children's Institute (2010) has applied this framework to early childhood care and education, specifically related to quality improvement:

Stage 1: Precontemplation—Not yet acknowledging that there is a habit or behavior (such as adults' behavior that interferes with or prevents learning in children or adults) that needs to be changed

Stage 2: Contemplation—Acknowledging that there is a habit or behavior that needs to be changed (such as for the highest quality instruction) but not yet ready or sure of wanting to make a change

Stage 3: Preparation—Getting ready to change

Stage 4: Action—Changing behavior or implementing the change

Stage 5: Maintenance—Maintaining the new behavior

In addition to these stages, Prochaska and DiClemente's (1983) Stages of Change model includes relapse (going back to the old behaviors) and transcendence (fully integrating the new behavior in a way that returning to the old habit would seem atypical or abnormal). We have used the Stages of Change model frequently with early childhood practitioners. They have found it very useful to understand that "relapsing" can be a normal part of a change process of any kind. One early childhood coach had found this especially helpful after she discovered that people in a center she worked with had gone back to their previous behaviors and was struggling to understand this.

In the first two stages, Precontemplation and Contemplation, the person who is the focus of change is ambivalent and possibly resistant to efforts to encourage change. The goals of these early stages are to resolve ambivalence and build intrinsic motivation to change. This will likely include education about the benefits of changing and the negative consequences of declining to change.

In the later stages when the person actually articulates change goals and starts planning and taking action, there will be increased talk about change and the envisioning of a future that includes the desired changes. In these stages, the focus shifts to strengthening the commitment to change and helping the person develop and implement a change plan.

Here is what you'll see when the person moves past the early stages:

- decreased resistance to change
- decreased discussion about the issue and a feeling of waiting for the next step
- a sense of resolution in which the person may seem more relaxed and unburdened about the issue
- increased change talk
- increased questions about change
- greater envisioning of a future that includes changing
- experimenting with possible change actions

This framework can help you identify a mismatch between the stage of change and the approaches to change you might be using and think about a different strategy. In the beginning of our professional development with coaches, we help them think about what stages of change the people they are working with are in and what types of strategies they have been using. People are often surprised to find that most of their "caseload" are in Precontemplation and that the strategies they have been using work best with someone at a later stage. How might the stages of change be helpful to you as you begin to adopt a collective leadership approach?

## We Forget There Are Different Types of Changes or Challenges

Ron Heifetz has written extensively on the difference between technical and adaptive problems/challenges and has developed a leadership framework called adaptive leadership (Heifetz, Grashow, and Linsky 2009). Technical problems tend to have simple solutions, while adaptive problems are more complex. If you don't know the difference between these, and you treat every challenge like it is technical, you will not be successful. The 2011 article "Collective Impact" by John Kania and Mark Kramer discussed the difference between technical and adaptive problems: "Some social problems are technical in that the problem is well defined, the answer is known in advance, and one or a few organizations have the ability to implement the solution. . . . Adaptive problems, by contrast, are complex, the answer is not known, and even if it were, no single entity has the resources or authority to bring about the necessary change" (Kania and Kramer 2011, 39).

Applying more technical solutions to an adaptive challenge will never get you to a solution. Rarely in these complex times is any situation are ever 100 percent technical. Elements of challenges/solutions may be technical, but most situations and challenges are either only adaptive or both adaptive and technical. Adopting collective leadership requires adaptive solutions, and recognizing that this will require time and persistence will be helpful as you begin your journey.

## We Forget Change Is a Process Rather Than an Event

In *Managing Transitions: Making the Most of Change* (2009), William Bridges presents a framework on transitions that can help people experiencing changes. The decision to adopt collective leadership is a change, and Bridges's framework can help you understand how you and those you work with may be experiencing this change. The transition framework distinguishes between a change, which is an event or series of events, and transitions, which are experienced individually as a result of a change. People experience a change at the same time, but they do not go through the phases of transition at the same time.

For example, there might be a budget reduction, which is a change. What happens as a result of the budget reduction may include staff layoffs, reduction of services, and other changes. According to Bridges, how people feel and respond to the change(s) will depend on how they proceed through the three phases of a transition: the Ending, Neutral Zone, and New Beginning. The Ending requires letting go of the idea of what things "were" before the change. Even positive changes set off transitions when they contain endings. In the Ending phase, some people might feel out of control, while others might feel excited for the change ahead. Regardless of how they feel about the change, people in this phase will discover that they need to let go of the "usual" way things were. During this time, it is important to respect all perspectives and reactions to the change.

In the second phase, the Neutral Zone, Bridges encourages people to focus on going forward rather than dwelling on the past. There is not yet a new identity or "way things are." In the Neutral Zone, people commonly feel lost, in limbo, uncertain, and even a bit chaotic. People experiencing this stage might feel anxious or even angry. Those charged with leading the group through change should remember to be patient and encourage the group to be patient with themselves. Building on and encouraging the optimism of anyone who might be feeling positive about the change can also be helpful.

In the New Beginning phase, people begin to see the change as "the way things are." They are beginning to be comfortable with the new way of being and have chosen to participate in building new processes and to accept the new environment. People may feel impatient for progress and hopeful about the future. This is a great time to celebrate successes. You may hear things like "I never thought we would see the end of this, but I'm realizing that we will be okay with what we have right now." Depending on the change and the transition, arriving at the New Beginning can take time. Remember to be patient with yourself and those in your group.

## We Forget That Competency Needs to Develop over Time

Uncertainty is uncomfortable for us as human beings. Our brains want to latch onto certainty, and seeking to change practices sets the stage for uncertainty. As adults, we are often used to feeling competent in our jobs. Deciding to experiment or make changes, even positive ones that we really want to make, can be challenging. The following model of competency development can help remind us of the natural learning curve when developing new competencies. This is different from the stages of change in that it describes a process for learning a skill, which is different from changing a habit or behavior.

You may already be familiar with the "four learning stages," also known as the "conscious competence learning model." While it isn't clear who developed this model, it has great value in conceptualizing the learning process (Cannon, Feinstein, and Friesen 2010). This model provides four stages of learning: unconscious incompetence, conscious incompetence, conscious competence, and unconscious competence. The theory is that people move from not knowing what they don't know to being aware of what they don't know but without having the skill to get there. Over time, they develop knowledge and skill about what they are trying to do and need to think about it to be successful. Finally, when it is "mastered," the person can perform the skill without thinking about it too much.

## How to Make Change Easier

Knowing that change may be more difficult than you think and the underlying reasons why can help you plan your experiments with collective leadership. Having the mind-set of experimentation and curiosity will help you try new things and encourage those around you to do the same.

## Cycles of Progress

Earlier in the book we mentioned what Frederic Laloux (2016) calls "sense and respond" (in contrast to predict and control). Sense and respond entails having both a destination and a goal and having flexibility to adapt specific actions in the moment. This means there is a need to engage in planning as well as in sensing and responding. It's a both/

and rather than an either/or situation. There are times and situations when linear action plans are useful and other times when sensing and responding during implementation is going to help. Having a framework that incorporates both is necessary. The following graphic, which we call "cycles of progress," can help groups by providing a visual of a process that can be used to experiment with new practices. The word *experiment* is chosen deliberately to allow people freedom to try things out without feeling like they made a mistake or failed if it doesn't work out right away, or at all. This process is not strictly linear; it allows for a process to be known in advance, while the topics chosen during each cycle can be decided as work proceeds, related to some overall goals. This "road map" can be used by a group of two or more people as they move toward the adoption of collective leadership practices.

## Cycles of Progress

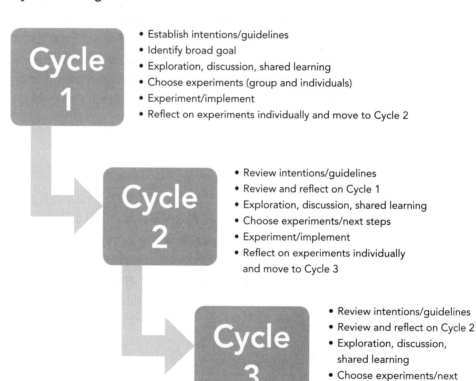

**Cycle 1**
- Establish intentions/guidelines
- Identify broad goal
- Exploration, discussion, shared learning
- Choose experiments (group and individuals)
- Experiment/implement
- Reflect on experiments individually and move to Cycle 2

**Cycle 2**
- Review intentions/guidelines
- Review and reflect on Cycle 1
- Exploration, discussion, shared learning
- Choose experiments/next steps
- Experiment/implement
- Reflect on experiments individually and move to Cycle 3

**Cycle 3**
- Review intentions/guidelines
- Review and reflect on Cycle 2
- Exploration, discussion, shared learning
- Choose experiments/next steps
- Experiment/implement
- Reflect on experiments individually
- Repeat

Cassandra was inspired to create this graphic for a group that had chosen to become a learning organization and was just beginning its journey. The group had met twice, with experiments in between. Someone in the group asked at the end of the second meeting, "I wonder what we accomplished?" Cassandra thought having a graphic of the process might help the group focus on its process and accomplishments, and the Cycles of Progress was born.

## Where Do I Go from Here?

Now what? At this point, you have all you need to start experimenting. What follows are some specific ways you can begin your experiments.

**Begin to adopt some collective leadership practices across the organization.** Identify practices that are already happening within the organization that are aligned with and contribute to collective leadership, reflect on what you want to do more of, brainstorm new ideas, and review collective leadership practices that others are using.

**Start a new group designed with a collective leadership model.** Maybe you are thinking about or planning to start a new group, learning community, community of practice, partnership, or coalition. You can design collective leadership practices into the way of operating from the beginning. This is probably the most ideal way to use a collective leadership model—from the outset, the values and practices will be in place.

**Within your existing programs, there may be opportunities to adopt collective leadership practices.** You and your staff may be mentoring or coaching participants in a way that is more directive than you want, or you may want to engage families in a different way. You can change how you work with others by adopting some new approaches and trying some new things—one step at a time.

**Share information about research and best practices related to adult growth and development, supporting change, and learning organizations.** There are myriad resources on topics related to collective leadership that you can use to share information with your team, group, or organization. We have included many of them in appendix A. A great way to begin conversations about collective leadership is to have a group read an article, such as the one we wrote called "Collective

Leadership: Activating the Gifts of Your Team" (Brinkerhoff, Murrieta, and O'Neill 2015), then discuss how the information in the article is similar to or different from existing practices and how the new approach might be beneficial to the group. Summarize the conversation with a few actions on how you might move toward using practices that are aligned with research and best practice.

If you've made it this far, congratulations! You have now explored the foundations of trust and the elements of collective leadership, you know what it looks like in the various roles of the ECE system, and you might even have some concrete ways you want to use it in your setting. You have been invited to think about some of the barriers related to change and have read about some ways to make change easier. Chapter 7 contains two case studies with examples of how an organization and a statewide partnership are using collective leadership.

We are excited to help ECE practitioners at all levels of our system think about how to work even more effectively with one another in support of all children. As we have said, our goals as a field are lofty; they are ambitious. There are many systems and institutions, and the recent emphasis on addressing the fragmentation of our field creates a perfect opportunity to use collective leadership.

We have resources and tools in the appendixes to help you on your journey. We wish you the best of luck and welcome hearing from you.

# Case Studies

We have provided two case studies in this chapter to show how collective leadership is being used at an organizational level and at a statewide level and to help you think about how it might look in your own setting. The first is a story about how Executive Director Jenny Volpe uses this approach in the organization Make Way for Books. The second is a story about how Terri Clark, Arizona Literacy Director for Read On Arizona, uses collective leadership in a statewide partnership focused on early literacy.

Before you begin this chapter, we encourage you to turn back to page 77 and review the table "Collective Leadership at a Glance." Next, have some paper handy so you can reflect on the following questions as you read each case study:

What elements from the table did you notice in the case study?
Which of the beliefs were held by the group or by Jenny or Terri?
What practices were used, either by the group or by Jenny or Terri?
Review what you wrote, circle one or two elements that you are curious about trying in your setting, and think about your underlying beliefs. What are some practices that might be helpful for reaching your shared goals?
You can also use the tool Trying Something New (or Different) Made Easier (see appendix B) to dive deeper in thinking about and planning how you might apply some ideas from these case studies to your own work or setting.

## Collective Leadership: Nonprofit Organization Leadership

### Jenny Volpe, Executive Director, Make Way for Books

Jenny Volpe has been the executive director at Make Way for Books for four years. Make Way for Books provides services and programs in Tucson, Arizona, to promote early literacy in the community. Jenny shares how she and her organization have used collective leadership:

> *Collective leadership is such a great fit because it is very much how we work in early childhood classrooms with children. Really effective leadership is similar to being a great teacher and running a really good classroom in that you always want to be building upon children's strengths (or in this case, your coworkers' and team's strengths), and recognize that everyone has something very unique and precious to offer. Collective leadership involves encouraging your team to recognize that it is in the differences and the multiplicity of voices that you get the best decisions, the best programs, and the best organizations.*
>
> *Collective leadership is at work at every level in our organization. The values aren't just a piece of paper; they guide what we do. We live and breathe these values and hold ourselves accountable to them. Our core values are centered on empowerment, and if we want to empower the community, we need to have staff who are also empowered. We have a culture and practices that incorporate all voices and include input from everyone that might be affected by the decisions and the work. For example, our core values were created and agreed upon by everyone at Make Way for Books. Their authenticity and ability to build a positive organizational culture come from the strength and diversity of the voices who proudly contributed to their creation. When it was time to revisit our strategic plan, we did it together. We got input from everyone—not just staff and our board, but volunteers, parents, and community members. It was a collective process. We took time to talk about our organizational culture and asked questions like "What is it about this culture that makes us unique and effective? How do we articulate it? What are our shared ideas of why we do this work, what matters most in how we achieve our mission?" We invited several stakeholders to these discussions, and it involved many meetings. Part of what made it successful was effectively including the voices of the*

*people who are affected by our programs and services. They were the most critical in the design of what we were going to do. So we invited parents, educators, and other community members and included them in the strategic-planning process. Getting meaningful input from people doesn't happen quickly! We had to be very intentional about the process and be sure that we had carefully crafted, open-ended questions that would help us learn what we were seeking to know. We had to think about what we wanted people to contribute and had to recognize that we wouldn't get done in two weeks. We had to allow ample time for the process.*

*We frequently use a similar process in our meetings for internal planning and for making adjustments to our services. Our program teams use an intentional, reflective process to identify what's going well, as well as what might need to change. We also make sure to get everyone at the table, including a parent representative. We will remind ourselves of the goal of the program and then we make sure that what we are doing is meeting our goal and is creating results. Our reflective process is driven by data and is all about commitment to continuous improvement. And what we learn might result in making changes or adaptations to our services.*

*Reflection is infused into our everyday work. Teams reflect, individuals reflect. We have weekly meetings where people share their responses to questions like "What were you proud of? How did you use your strengths? What is challenging? What did you discover about yourself and your work? What are you most grateful for?" What we are finding is that by building a reflective culture, we uncover people's strengths, and the work becomes deeper and more meaningful. And because our organization is adaptable and flexible, we are able to shift tasks and sometimes even job descriptions so people have more opportunities to use their strengths. For example, we hired a grant writer, and it quickly became apparent that she was very creative and good at graphic design as well and really enjoyed doing it. So her job title and tasks were changed so she could do both things, and she does very well at both. She also values that our organization recognized her strengths and interests, and allowed her to further develop her skills and put them to greater use.*

*Our annual reviews are a culmination of the ongoing reflection that has been occurring daily, weekly, and monthly all year. They build on strengths and involve a supervisor and employee reflecting together on that employee's particular successes. Employees reflect on* what challenges they overcame and what they were particularly proud of achieving, and talk about their own growth. This is very different from more traditional reviews where you may focus on a person's gaps. I'm getting feedback on this process that people really appreciate the opportunity and ability to reflect. They value the time dedicated to ongoing reflection. The richness and depth resulting from thinking about the growth throughout the year really provides people an opportunity to think about how they want to grow next.

Something that has helped this collective work for us is to have good hiring processes. When you hire a person, you need to make sure they are a good fit. Do they share the values and are they willing to make a commitment to uphold the values and the culture? Another thing that is important is to be willing to address conflict directly. It takes courage to hold people accountable to their agreement to be fully part of the culture. Nobody likes conflict, but it does come up, and it is critical to be able to remind people about the agreements when it is needed. That's why having authentic core values is such an important part of building our positive work culture. Everyone knows how we have agreed to go about our important work together and in the community.

I've learned that it is really important to have a common vision and also not to assume that everyone is on board with it. It's important to make the time to articulate the vision together, to make sure it is stated, and that there is a common language. You also need to be very good at self-reflection. Leading in this way is nuanced, and there are hard things you have to master—you need to be willing to work on yourself. You need to develop your own emotional intelligence and learn to recognize your biases and how they affect your perspective. And you need to learn how to help other people do the same. But it is exciting! This approach builds trust and meaningful relationships, and I think it can be used to create multiorganizational, collective change. It might even change funding down the road and could even shift the design of social programs and initiatives in the future.

# Collective Leadership: Statewide Partnership

### Terri Clark, Arizona Literacy Director, Read On Arizona

Terri Clark is the director of a statewide collective impact initiative called Read On Arizona. Its mission is to help communities increase their early literacy rates, with the long-term goal of increasing third-grade reading proficiency levels across the state. The initiative is a public/private partnership of over one hundred organizations and twenty communities. Terri shares how she and the partners have used collective leadership:

> Trust has been critical. In the beginning, it was crucial to build trust with our partners. One of the ways we did that was to focus on projects that would demonstrate results and show our willingness to be accountable. A specific example is our Early Literacy Guide. This guide was collectively written with the State Board of Education and the State Department of Education. We wrote the guide to address a gap around what families knew about the recent legislation Move On When Reading. We also wanted to be sure that families knew about the importance of early literacy. The Read On partners worked with the state agency partners to create this shared project. In this way, we were able to demonstrate that we have a shared goal of promoting early literacy, that we had a shared message around how families could support their children's early literacy, and that we valued collaboration. Cocreating the guide helped build trust with the state: they knew they could trust us as partners.
>
> Another example of how trust is central to our work was our Data Integration and Systems Task Force. We knew that there were multiple agencies that held data related to early literacy. Our goal was to find a way to make data related to early literacy more accessible so the community could use data to make decisions. We started to have conversations about sharing data, and as you can imagine, when those kinds of conversations begin, walls can go up. People get nervous and sometimes question intentions, and trust becomes even more crucial. The group knew what the vision was, they knew what was needed, and there were definitely challenges and issues to work through. But as we worked through the barriers together and had those tough

*conversations, trust was strengthened. What we were able to produce was beyond anyone's initial vision: we have created an early literacy data center. The data center includes an interactive and publicly accessible data mapping tool that can be used to help the community make decisions about services based on relevant data. This process wasn't easy, and we went the extra mile to show our commitment to maintaining trust by creating an "Intended Use" agreement for the data center so users are required to agree to use the data in a way that matches what the partners intended. This document provided assurance to the partners, which also helped strengthen trust.*

*Trust is multilayered, and it rests on the confidence that people are going to do what they say they are going to do. Trust is broken when people don't honor their commitments. So for myself, I need to be sure that I follow through with what I say I'm going to do. And when there are times when a partner doesn't follow through on a commitment, I need to be sure to frame the conversation in a positive and solution-focused way while still expecting accountability and follow through. This includes assuming that others have positive intentions and are not just falling back on assumptions. I'll ask, "What can we do next time so we can realize the outcome we want to see?"*

*This kind of work requires levels of partnership that go beyond just making decisions and informing partners. It requires that people aren't just shaking their heads without their full buy-in and commitment to take action. To support this, we went through a year-long leadership training on Results-Based Leadership and Results-Based Accountability. The program focused on developing leadership to be more action oriented and is framed around results and data. To us, results-based accountability means that when things aren't going as planned, and we aren't seeing the results we want to see, we make sure we stop and figure out why and readjust if needed.*

*Results- and data-centered focus has been helpful. When results and data are at the center, it takes the emotion and the subjectivity out of it. We need to be able to look at the data about a strategy and say, "Because of that, something is different." I also remind myself and the partners not to fall in love with the strategy but to fall in love with the results. I often say, "No strategy is safe." Focusing on results and data takes patience, as you can't always see the immediate result. You need to be patient without being passive. I'm often reminding partners,*

*"Don't just do something because it's what you've always done; do it because it is showing results."*

*What I've learned as a leader in this collective impact initiative is that collaboration is hard. It is difficult. But it should be. When we get uncomfortable, that's often when we are on the cusp of change and improvement. Results and data keep people focused and on the "developmental edge." When we have the most discomfort, it probably means that we are closer to accelerating results. We need to stay on that edge and out of the comfort zone if we are really going to create change.*

# Appendix A: Resources

## General Resources

The following references can be useful in adopting collective leadership:

**Aspen Institute, Ascend Initiative Supporting Two-Generation Strategies** (http://ascend.aspeninstitute.org). This Aspen Institute Initiative offers resources on how to effectively engage families and how programs and funders can focus on the whole family by providing workforce development services to the parents to increase the income of the family while providing high-quality early childhood services for young children. It operates a network of organizations committed to these approaches.

**Aspen Institute, Dialogue on Public Libraries** (http://csreports .aspeninstitute.org/Dialogue-on-Public-Libraries/2015/library). This Aspen Institute Initiative offers resources on transforming libraries, which is helpful for early childhood partnerships and community engagement.

**Build Initiative** (www.buildinitiative.org). The Build Initiative offers resources on system building to support early childhood development and resources specific to quality improvement in early childhood settings.

**The Center for Evolutionary Leadership** (http://evolutionleader.com). The Center for Evolutionary Leadership offers resources on new thinking about leadership that is aligned with collective leadership.

**Collective Leadership Self-Assessment** (www.stakeholderdialogues .net/learning/toolbox/collective-leadership-self-assessment). This online assessment assesses your group's collective leadership skills and path forward.

**Harvard University Center on the Developing Child, Collective Change** (http://developingchild.harvard.edu/collective-change). This initiative for collective action provides resources for early childhood collective leadership.

**Leadership Learning Community** (http://leadershiplearning.org). This website has extensive leadership resources, including reports and webinars on shared leadership, addressing white privilege, and complexity.

**Polarity Partnerships** (www.polaritypartnerships.com). Here you'll find resources on how to think in a both/and way, rather than either/or, when looking at polarities or competing commitments that may affect groups.

**Project Implicit, Implicit Bias Test** (http://implicit.harvard.edu /implicit/takeatest.html). This online test can help increase your awareness of your own implicit bias.

**Waters Foundation, Systems Thinking in Education** (http://watersfoundation.org). This website has resources to help educators utilize system thinking tools.

**Wilder Collaboration Factors Inventory** (http://wilderresearch.org /tools/cfi/index.php). This online collaboration tool helps groups assess different aspects of how they are working together.

Glaser, Judith E. 2014. *Conversational Intelligence: How Great Leaders Build Trust and Get Extraordinary Results*. New York: Bibliomotion.

Kanter, Beth, and Allison H. Fine. 2010. *The Networked Nonprofit: Connecting with Social Media to Drive Change*. San Francisco: Jossey-Bass.

Kanter, Beth, and Katie Delahaye Paine. 2012. *Measuring the Networked Nonprofit: Using Data to Change the World*. San Francisco: Jossey-Bass.

Meehan, Deborah, Claire Reinelt, and Sally Leiderman. 2015. "Leadership and Large-Scale Change: How to Accelerate Learning and Deepen Impact." Leadership Learning Community, June.

Sagarin, Rafe. 2012. *Learning from the Octopus: How Secrets from Nature Can Help Us Fight Terrorist Attacks, Natural Disasters, and Disease*. New York: Basic Books.

Sharken Simon, Judith. 2001. *The Five Life Stages of Nonprofit Organizations: Where You Are, Where You're Going, and What to Expect When You Get There*. St. Paul, MN: Amherst H. Wilder Foundation.

Wheatley, Margaret. 1999. "Core Practices of Life-Affirming Leaders." The Berkana Institute. http://berkana.org/wp-content/uploads/2011/11/New_CorePracticesofLifeAffirmingLeaders.pdf.

## Collective Leadership Practices

### Adopt a Mind-set of Abundance

**The Inquiry Institute Choice Map** (http://inquiryinstitute.com). The Inquiry Institute is a consulting, coaching, and educational organization founded by Marilee Adams (PhD) that has several resources to help individuals and groups switch from a judger to a learner mind-set, including the Choice Map.

**Mindset** (www.mindsetonline.com). Carol S. Dweck has researched the growth and fixed mind-set. The website includes a way to test your mindset and four simple steps to start changing your mind-set.

Kanter, Beth, and Aliza Sherman. 2017. *The Happy, Healthy Nonprofit: Strategies for Impact without Burnout.* Hoboken, NJ: Wiley.

Twist, Lynne. 2006. *The Soul of Money: Reclaiming the Wealth of Our Inner Resources.* New York: W. W. Norton.

### Engage in Reflection and Application of Learning

**Center for Evaluation Innovation** (www.evaluationinnovation.org). This website offers innovative resources on evaluating things that are complicated, such as advocacy, system change, and networks.

Gill, Stephen J. 2009. *Developing a Learning Culture in Nonprofit Organizations.* Thousand Oaks, CA: Sage Publications.

### Identify and Build on Strengths

**Appreciative Inquiry Commons** (https://appreciativeinquiry.case.edu). The Appreciative Inquiry Commons offers resources from all over the world on using Appreciative Inquiry, a strengths-based approach to change.

**StandOut Assessment** (https://www.tmbc.com). Access information about this strengths assessment tool created by Marcus Buckingham that identifies your top strengths so you can take action.

**StrengthsFinder** (www.strengthsfinder.com/home.aspx). This website includes information about the strengths assessment tool created by Gallup and the research on strengths.

Cooperrider Dole, Dawn, Jen Hetzel Silbert, Ada Jo Mann, and Diana Whitney. 2008. *Positive Family Dynamics: Appreciative Inquiry Questions to Bring Out the Best in Families.* Chagrin Falls, OH: Taos Institute Publications.

Jablon,Judy, Amy Laura Dombro, and Shaun Johnsen. 2014. *Coaching with Powerful Interactions: A Guide for Partnering with Early Childhood Teachers.* Washington, DC: NAEYC.

Rath, Tom. 2007. *StrengthsFinder 2.0.* New York: Gallup Press.

———. 2008. *Strengths Based Leadership.* New York: Gallup Press.

Whitney, Diana, Amanda Trosten-Bloom, Jay Cherney, and Ron Fry. 2004. *Appreciative Team Building: Positive Questions to Bring Out the Best of Your Team.* Lincoln, NE: iUniverse.

## Identify Shared Goals

**SOAR Strategy** (www.soar-strategy.com). Find resources on conducting strengths-based strategic planning and using the SOAR approach (strengths, opportunities, aspirations, and results) here. This model is an alternative to the SWOT assessment sometimes used (strengths, weaknesses, opportunities, and threats).

Stavros, Jacqueline M., and Gina Hinrichs. 2009. *The Thin Book of SOAR: Building Strengths-Based Strategy.* Bend, OR: Thin Book Publishing.

## Make Agreements / Adopt Structures of Accountability

**Results-Based Accountability Guide** (http://raguide.org). This website has resources and information for facilitators using Results-Based Accountability. There are techniques, tools, and exercises as well as an implementation overview.

Pruitt, Deborah. 2012. *Group Alchemy: The Six Elements of Highly Successful Collaboration*. Emeryville, CA: Group Alchemy Publishing.

## Practice Self-Care and Build Resiliency

**Beth's Blog** (www.bethkanter.org). Beth Kanter's site includes resources and blog posts on a wide range of topics that align with increasing effectiveness and resiliency building.

**The Deveraux Center for Resilient Children** (www.centerfor resilientchildren.org). This website has resources for building resiliency in children and adults, including a resiliency assessment for adults.

Neff, Kristin. 2016. "Don't Fall into the Self-Esteem Trap: Try a Little Self-Kindness." *Mindful*, February 17. www.mindful.org /dont-fall-into-the-self-esteem-trap-try-a-little-self-kindness.

## Provide and Elicit Feedback That Promotes Growth and Development

**Austin's Butterfly** (https://vimeo.com/38247060). This six-minute video is a great resource about the results that are possible when positive and specific feedback is provided.

Pink, Daniel. 2010. "Think Tank: Fix the Workplace, Not the Workers." *Daily Telegraph*, November 6. www.telegraph.co.uk/finance /jobs/8113600/Think-Tank-Fix-the-workplace-not-the-workers.html.

## Rotate and/or Share Roles and Responsibilities

Gill, Stephen. 2009. *Developing a Learning Culture in Nonprofit Organizations*. Thousand Oaks, CA: Sage Publications.

## Skillfully Navigate Difficult Conversations and Conflict

**Conflict Climate Inventory** (www.conflictclimate.com). This website includes an assessment tool that can be used to identify how conflict is affecting an organization.

**Style Matters Conflict Style Inventory** (http://www.riverhouseepress
.com). The website includes an assessment that shows users their pre-
ferred conflict style.

Abrams, Jennifer. 2009. *Having Hard Conversations*. Thousand Oaks,
CA: Corwin.

———. 2016. *Having Hard Conversations Unpacked: The Whos, the
Whens, and the What-Ifs*. Thousand Oaks, CA: Corwin.

Fisher, Roger, William Ury, and Bruce Patton. 2011. *Getting to Yes:
Negotiating Agreement without Giving In*. Rev. ed. New York: Penguin.


## Use Effective Facilitation and Engagement Strategies That Activate Collective Wisdom/Intelligence

**Liberating Structures: Including and Unleashing Everyone** (www
.liberatingstructures.com/ls-menu). This website lists many different
facilitation methods and meeting strategies that liberate energy and
collective wisdom.

Butler, Ava S. 2014. *Mission Critical Meetings: 81 Practical Facilitation
Techniques*. Tucson, AZ: Wheatmark.

Lipmanowicz, Henri, and Keith McCandless. 2014. *The Surprising Power
of Liberating Structures: Simple Rules to Unleash a Culture of Innovation*.
Seattle: Liberating Structures Press.


## Use Structures and Processes for Effective and Shared Decision Making

**RACI Charts** (http://racichart.org). RACI charts are decision or task
matrices that clarify roles and responsibilities.

Heath, Chip, and Dan Heath. 2013. *Decisive: How to Make Better
Choices in Life and Work*. New York: Crown Business.

Kaner, Sam. 2014. *Facilitator's Guide to Participatory Decision-Making*.
3rd ed. San Francisco: Jossey-Bass.

# Appendix B: Tools

## Tool 1: Appreciative Inquiry Interview Guide

An Appreciative Inquiry Interview Guide is useful in helping people discover things that are going well, reconnect with positive and inspiring experiences they have had, and hear about these kinds of experiences from others. These types of questions help people connect with aspirations that are visionary and motivating, especially when they are shared by a group, team, organization, and community. The questions below can be used in many ways: as a regular agenda item in your meetings and during retreats and planning processes or any time you want to invite people to discover or rediscover something positive about themselves and others.

One way to use this interview guide in a meeting is to have people pair off and interview each other. If you have enough time, you can build on this by having people stay with their partners and join another pair, resulting in small groups of four. You can then have people share the highlights of what they heard from their partners with the small group and capture the highlights of the small group on a flip chart to share with the whole group.

These simple questions are truly magical and can transform the vibrancy of your meetings and the future for you and your team. Appreciative inquiry has been around since the 1980s, and many resources are available if you are interested in learning more, including books that contain appreciative interview questions on different topics (listed in appendix A), and we have provided additional interview guides for ECE practitioners on the Redleaf Press website (www .redleafpress.org).

# Appreciative Interview Guide

Instructions:
- Each person will find a partner. The pair will choose a person A and B.
- Round 1: Person A will go first and ask Person B all the questions on the interview guide.
- Person A will listen. When the questions are all asked and answered, the roles will change. You will have about ten minutes per person for the interviews.
- If you finish before the ten minutes are up, feel free to switch roles.
- Round 2: Person B will ask Person A the same questions and listen to the answers.

Tell me a story about a peak experience that you had at work when you were contributing meaningfully, a time you felt alive, excited, and engaged.

Without being modest, what was your contribution to this experience? What do you value most about

- yourself;

- your team; and

- your organization?

Imagine it's five years from now and your organization has built on the strengths to reach shared aspirations. The staff, families, and the communities you serve are thriving. Your organization makes a tremendous difference. What does this look like? What new things are you doing? What were the first steps you took that paved the way for the incredible results you have achieved?

What three wishes do you have for your organization and community?

This section is for taking notes on your partner's story. If there is time, record your answers to the following prompts for each interview:

Great quotes from the interview:

What inspired you?

What surprised you?

Notes on story:

Notes on future vision:

## Tool 2: Trying Something New (or Different) Made Easier

Adopt the mind-set of an experimenter. We know it's not always easy to try something new or different; habits are hard to break, and trying something new can be uncomfortable or scary because you don't know what will happen and you might not be good at a new thing the first time you try it.

This tool can make trying something new or making a change easier. Having a plan makes trying something new or different both easier and more likely. When this tool is used in groups during meetings or trainings, you can be sure that people will try something afterward—especially if they know that they will be coming back and sharing how it went.

Another reason this tool is helpful is the planned reflection time. Trying something new might not work as you hope the first time, and knowing there is a time set aside to reflect on how the process went takes some pressure off. The planned reflection gives an opportunity to think about what could be done differently when you try something new or different again. This can help people recover quickly or try something else if the process wasn't "perfect" the first time.

If you think specifically about when and how you are going to try something, you will be more likely to try it. Say you were reading this book and you learned about several tools and resources that you thought you might try. After considering three things, you select one thing to try and make a plan to use it. Below are the questions from the first section of the tool, and an example of what it looks like when it's filled out.

Planning questions to answer before trying something new or different:

1. What are two or three things you want to try? **Answer:** Using the Choice Map (see appendix A), using questions that build on strengths (see Tool 3 in appendix B), and using the core practices of life-affirming leaders (see appendix A).

2. What are some situations in the next week or two in which you would be able to try using these? **Answer:** In the next two weeks, I will be going to a staff meeting that I could bring something to, I

will have a coaching session with a teacher I'm working with, and I could reflect about a situation that I'm finding challenging.

3. Which one specifically would you like to plan on doing? **Answer:** I am going to journal about how I could use the learner and judger mind-set questions in the Choice Map to help myself with a challenging situation. I plan on journaling Monday at the end of work.

4. What could you do to make it easier or more likely that you will actually do this? **Answer:** I'll put it in my calendar for a specific time on Monday.

5. Anything else that will help you? **Answer:** I could ask someone else to do it with me. I will think about this.

6. When will you plan to answer the reflecting questions about what happened? **Answer:** I will plan to answer the reflecting questions on Tuesday at the end of work.

Once you've done your experiment and tried what you had planned in your answers above, answer the following reflecting questions.

Reflecting questions to answer after trying something new or different:

If you tried what you had planned, what happened? How did it go?

Was it like you thought it would be, or was it different? If it was different, how was it different?

How do you feel about what happened when you tried this new or different thing?

What did you discover from trying this? How was it helpful?

Do you want to try this again or try something else?

Any other comments?

Try using this tool

- by yourself
- when coaching
- with groups in meetings or trainings—have everyone fill it out (pick something and make a plan to try it), and have each person report back to the group what happened with their experiments

## Success Story

Jen Maney, who works at the Pima County (Arizona) Public Library, tells how she used this form to solve a time-management problem:

*When I originally thought of what I'd like to try, I thought about how distracted and interrupted I feel at work. I wanted a culprit for this, so I blamed e-mail. My original plan was to only check e-mail at two designated times per day and close it at all other times. This quickly proved impractical because I keep to-do items and action information in my e-mail for reference. I had a conversation with a coworker about different areas of performance, and we used a tool call the Performance Wheel to rate ourselves on different areas. I rated myself lower on time management than other areas, and armed with my new knowledge that e-mail wasn't the culprit, I devised a new plan.*

*My plan was to ask any person who came to "interrupt" me exactly how much time they needed and tell them how much time I realistically had. If they said they needed more than a couple of minutes, I'd ask them to schedule a separate meeting. I would do this for a week to see how much of my time it freed up. (Ah, the freedom I anticipated was great!) My prompt reminder was a sticky note on my monitor that says, "Do you have a minute?" I dutifully put the sticky note on my monitor and waited for the hordes to come in and interrupt me.*

*And yet, there were no hordes. Was it a quiet week? Not really. I had the normal amount of weekly activity as always. Was my plan working? Sure, people came in to talk with me sometimes, but there were not that many, and I wasn't irritated by any of them. And when I forgot to ask, "Is it really only a minute?" (which I did a lot), these interruptions didn't suck up my day. I realized that my perception of how many interruptions I get in a day far exceeded the reality. Giving myself the permission to ask the question and knowing I had a tool to use if I felt the need gave me the freedom I was looking for. I didn't use my tactic on every person, because their questions really were quick! I felt like I had mastered the interruptions. At the end of the week, I had put on my calendar a reminder to answer the second set of questions on the tool. I wrote, "I expected to have to use it a lot, and I didn't, which makes me think that interruptions aren't a big problem. It helped me feel in control of my time."*

*This was really eye-opening, and I wouldn't have even tried to address my feelings about interruptions without the tool. Makes me wonder what else I need to examine a little more closely.*

The questions on the next page can be copied and used with individuals or groups to help make a plan to try something new and then return to reflect on the experience afterward.

# Trying Something New (or Different) Made Easier

1.  What are two or three things you want to try?

2.  What are some situations in the next week or two in which you would be able to try using these?

3.  Which one specifically would you like to plan on doing?

4.  What could you do to make it easier or more likely that you will actually do this?

5.  Anything else that will help you?

6.  When will you plan to answer the reflecting questions about what happened?

7.  Did you try the new or different thing as you had planned? If yes, move on to reflecting questions. If no, what got in the way? Do you want to try this again or try something else? Make your decision and then answer the questions above and add an additional question: What might get in the way when you try this, and how can you prepare for this?

8. Reflecting questions to answer after trying something new or different:

9. If you tried what you had planned, what happened? How did it go?

10. Was it like you thought it would be, or was it different? If it was different, how was it different?

11. How do you feel about what happened when you tried this new or different thing?

12. What did you discover from trying this? How was it helpful?

13. Do you want to try this again or something else?

Any other comments?

## Tool 3: Questions That Identify and Build on Strengths

Are you looking for ways to identify and build on the strengths of people you supervise, coach, or collaborate with? Sometimes we forget to do the simplest step first: ask! Usually, what people say they enjoy doing is also something they are good at. Once you find out what people's gifts are, you can think about ways in which those gifts might fit into your team or project how their strengths can help support success in something you are focusing on during coaching. Some questions you can ask:

- What are some thing things that others have said you are good at doing?
- What are things that you really enjoy doing (maybe you enjoy doing them so much that you even lose track of time while engaged in the activity)?
- What are you passionate about?

Combining the strengths people verbalize along with pointing out strengths that you notice along the way can be a powerful way to uncover hidden potential. Once that gets matched to actions and tasks going forward, you will be on your way to helping those around you develop their strengths.

We have provided a tool on the next page that could be used during a staff meeting with someone you supervise. It could also be used with groups to promote reflection and evolution. Tip: It's often easier for people to write the answers to the questions first, before having a conversation about them.

# Questions That Identify and Build on Strengths

1. Talk about a success you have had since we last met.

2. What were some things you did to contribute to the success?

3. What ideas do you have to use the strengths you mentioned (read the person's response to question 2 to remind them of their strengths) in the near future? (How can the strengths be applied to another situation, project, or setting?)

4. What is something you learned since we last met?

5. How might you apply that learning to another similar situation coming up?

6. What do you want to remember from our conversation?

# References

Abel, Mike, Teri Talan, and Marie Masterson. 2017. "Whole Leadership."
  *Exchange*, January/February.

Alinsky, Saul. 1971. *Rules for Radicals: A Practical Primer for Realistic Radicals.*
  New York: Random House.

*American Heritage Dictionary Online.* 2017a. "Power." Accessed May 15. https
  ://ahdictionary.com/word/search.html?q=power.

———. 2017b. "Privilege." Accessed May 15. https://ahdictionary.com/word
  /search.html?q=privilege.

Arrien, Angeles. 1993. *The Four-Fold Way: Walking the Paths of the Warrior,
  Teacher, Healer, and Visionary.* New York: HarperCollins.

Asplund, Jim, and Nikki Blacksmith. 2011. "How Strengths Boost Engagement."
  *Gallup Business Journal*, April 7. www.gallup.com/businessjournal/146972
  /strengths-boost-engagement.aspx.

Bolden, Richard. 2011. "Distributed Leadership in Organizations: A Review of
  Theory and Research." *International Journal of Management Reviews* 13 (3):
  251–69. doi:10.1111/j.1468-2370.2011.00306.

Bridges, William. 2009. *Managing Transitions: Making the Most of Change.* 3rd
  ed. Philadelphia: Da Capo Press.

Brinkerhoff, Monica, Albert Murrieta, and Cassandra O'Neill. 2015. "Collective
  Leadership: Activating the Gifts of Your Team." *Exchange* (November/
  December): 51–54.

Bronfenbrenner, Urie. 1992. "Ecological Systems Theory." In *Six Theories of
  Child Development: Revised Formulations and Current Issues*, edited by Ross
  Vasta, 187–250. London: Jessica Kingsley Publishers.

Brown, Brené. 2012. *Daring Greatly: How the Courage to Be Vulnerable
  Transforms the Way We Live, Love, Parent, and Lead.* New York: Gotham.

Cabaj, Mark, and Liz Weaver. 2016. "Collective Impact 3.0: An Evolving
  Framework for Community Change." Tamarack Institute. https://
  collectiveimpactforum.org/sites/default/files/Collective%20Impact
  %203.0.pdf.

Cannon, Hugh M., Andrew H. Feinstein, and Daniel P. Friesen. 2010. "Managing Complexity: Applying the Conscious-Competence Model to Experiential Learning." *Developments in Business Simulation and Experiential Learning* 37: 172–82.

Castle, Victoria. 2006. *The Trance of Scarcity: Stop Holding Your Breath and Start Living Your Life*. San Francisco: Berrett-Koehler.

Cheung, Rebecca, and W. Norton Grubb. 2014. *Collective and Team Leadership: Preparation for Urban Schools*. University of California, Berkeley. https://principals.berkeley.edu/sites/default/files/PLI_Collective_and_Team_Leadership_0.pdf.

Children's Institute. 2010. "Readiness Scale Gains National Attention." *Children's Institute News and Views*, Spring 2010. www.childrensinstitute.net/sites/default/files/documents/newsletter-2010.pdf.

Collaboration for Impact. 2017. "The Collective Impact Framework." www.collaborationforimpact.com/collective-impact.

Costa, Arthur L., and Robert J. Garmston. 2002. *Cognitive Coaching: A Foundation for Renaissance Schools*. 2nd ed. Norwood, MA: Christopher-Gordon Publishers.

Covey, Stephen M. R. 2006. *The Speed of Trust: The One Thing That Changes Everything*. With Rebecca R. Merrill. New York: Free Press.

Cramer, Kathryn D., and Hank Wasiak. 2006. *Change the Way You See Everything through Asset-Based Thinking*. Philadelphia, PA: Running Press.

Crutchfield, Leslie R., and Heather McLeod Grant. 2008. *Forces for Good: The Six Practices of High-Impact Nonprofits*. San Francisco: Jossey-Bass.

DeMatthews, David. 2016. "Effective Leadership Is Not Enough: Critical Approaches to Closing the Racial Discipline Gap." *The Clearing House: A Journal of Educational Strategies, Issues and Ideas* 89 (1): 7–13.

Derman-Sparks, Louise, Debbie LeeKeenan, and John Nimmo. 2014. *Leading Anti-Bias Early Childhood Programs: A Guide for Change*. New York: Teachers College Press; Washington, DC: NAEYC.

Di Stefano, Giada, Francesca Gino, Gary Pisano, and Bradley Staats. 2014. "Learning by Thinking: How Reflection Improves Performance." Working Knowledge, Harvard Business School. http://hbswk.hbs.edu/item/learning-by-thinking-how-reflection-improves-performance.

Duarte, Nancy, and Patti Sanchez. 2016. *Illuminate: Ignite Change through Speeches, Stories, Ceremonies, and Symbols*. New York: Penguin.

Dweck, Carol S. 2006. *Mindset: The New Psychology of Success*. New York: Ballantine Books.

Fox, Elliot M., and L. Urwick. 1973. *Dynamic Administration: The Collected Papers of Mary Parker Follett*. Rev. ed. London: Pitman.

Freire, Paulo. 1970. *Pedagogy of the Oppressed*. New York: Seabury Press.

Freiwirth, Judy. 2007. *Engagement Governance for System-Wide Decision Making.* *Nonprofit Quarterly*, Summer 2007. http://nonprofnetwork.org/Resources /Documents/Resources/Engagement%20Governance%20NonQtrly07.pdf.

Fuda, Peter, and Richard Badham. 2011. "Fire, Snowball, Mask, Movie: How Leaders Spark and Sustain Change." *Harvard Business Review*, November. https://hbr.org/2011/11/fire-snowball-mask-movie-how-leaders-spark -and-sustain-change.

Fullan, Michael. 2013. *Maximizing Leadership for Change.* http://www .michaelfullan.ca/wp-content/uploads/2013/10/13_Australia-Maximizing-Leadership-for-Change_Part-1.pdf.

Galinsky, Ellen. 2010. *Mind in the Making: The Seven Essential Life Skills Every Child Needs.* New York: Harper Studio.

Gill, Stephen J. 2009. *Developing a Learning Culture in Nonprofit Organizations.* Thousand Oaks, CA: Sage Publications.

Glaser, Judith E. 2014. *Conversational Intelligence: How Great Leaders Build Trust and Get Extraordinary Results.* New York: Bibliomotion.

Goffin, Stacie G. 2013. *Early Childhood Education for a New Era: Leading for Our Profession.* New York: Teachers College Press.

———. 2015. *Professionalizing Early Childhood Education As a Field of Practice: A Guide to the Next Era.* St. Paul, MN: Redleaf Press.

Goffin, Stacie G., and Valora Washington. 2007. *Ready or Not: Leadership Choices in Early Care and Education.* New York: Teachers College Press.

Harvard Family Research Project. 2015. "Taking the Lead in Family Engagement: A Message to Our Followers on President's Day." February 13. www.hfrp.org/publications-resources/browse-our-publications/taking-the -lead-in-family-engagement-a-message-to-our-followers-on-presidents-day.

Harvard University Center on the Developing Child. 2017. "Distributed Leadership." http://developingchild.harvard.edu/collective-change /key-concepts/distributed-leadership.

Heath, Chip, and Dan Heath. 2011. *Switch: How to Change Things When Change Is Hard.* New York: Broadway Books.

Heifetz, Ronald, Alexander Grashow, Marty Linsky. 2009. *The Practice of Adaptive Leadership: Tools and Tactics for Changing Your Organization and the World.* Boston: Harvard Business Press.

Institute of Medicine and National Research Council. 2015. *Transforming the Workforce for Children Birth through Age 8: A Unifying Foundation.* Washington, DC: National Academies Press. www.nap.edu/catalog/19401 /transforming-the-workforce-for-children-birth-through-age-8-a.

Kania, John, and Mark Kramer. 2011. "Collective Impact." *Stanford Social Innovation Review.* https://ssir.org/articles/entry/collective_impact.

Kanter, Beth. 2017. "What Does Resiliency Really Mean for Nonprofit Leaders and Their Organizations?" *Beth's Blog.* January 5. www.bethkanter.org /nonprofit-resilience.

Kanter, Beth, and Aliza Sherman. 2017. *The Happy, Healthy Nonprofit: Strategies for Impact without Burnout.* Hoboken, NJ: Wiley.

Kegan, Robert, and Lisa Lahey. 2016. "An Everyone Culture: Becoming a Deliberately Developmental Organization." *Stanford Social Innovation Review.* April 6. https://ssir.org/articles/entry/an_everyone_culture_becoming_a_deliberately_developmental_organization.

Kellogg Leadership for Community Change. 2008. *Collective Leadership Works: Preparing Youth and Adults for Community Change.* http://theinnovationcenter.org/files/file/Collective-Leadership-ALL-LINKS.pdf.

Kuenkel, Petra, and Kristiane Schaefer. 2013. *Shifting the Way We Co-Create. How We Can Change the Challenges of Sustainability into Opportunities.* Vol. 1, *Collective Leadership Studies.* http://stakeholderdialogues.net/media/uploads/Collective_Leadership_Studies_Vol1-Shifting_the_Way_We_Co-create.pdf.

Laloux, Frederic. 2014. *Reinventing Organizations: A Guide to Creating Organizations Inspired by the Next Stage of Human Consciousness.* Brussels, Belgium: Nelson Parker.

———. 2016. *Reinventing Organizations: An Illustrated Invitation to Join the Conversation on Next-Stage Organizations.* Brussels, Belgium: Nelson Parker.

Leadership Learning Community. 2010. *Leadership and Race: How to Develop and Support Leadership That Contributes to Racial Justice.* http://leadershiplearning.org/system/files/Leadership%20and%20Race%20FINAL_Electronic_072010.pdf.

Lee, Kien. 2007. *The Importance of Culture in Evaluation: A Practical Guide for Evaluators.* The Colorado Trust. www.communityscience.com/pdfs/CrossCulturalGuide.r3.pdf.

Lewin-Benham, Ann. 2011. *Twelve Best Practices for Early Childhood Education: Integrating Reggio and Other Inspired Approaches.* New York: Teachers College Press.

MacDonald, Susan. 2016. *Inspiring Early Childhood Leadership: Eight Strategies to Ignite Passion and Transform Program Quality.* Lewisville, NC: Gryphon House.

McIntosh, Peggy. 2010. "Some Notes for Facilitators on Presenting My White Privilege Papers." https://nationalseedproject.org/white-privilege-unpacking-the-invisible-knapsack.

McNeish, Robert. 1972. "Lessons from Geese." http://terrygossassoc.com/PDF_Lessons_from_Geese.pdf.

Meehan, Deborah, and Claire Reinelt. 2012. *Leadership and Networks: New Ways of Developing Leadership in a Highly Connected World.* Leadership Learning Community. http://leadershiplearning.org/system/files/LLCNetworkNLfinal4.pdf.

NAEYC (National Association for the Education of Young Children). 2011. *Code of Ethical Conduct and Statement of Commitment.* www.naeyc.org/files /naeyc/file/positions/PSETH05.pdf.

National Opportunity to Learn Campaign. 2014. *Restorative Practices: Fostering Healthy Relationships & Promoting Positive Discipline in Schools, A Guide for Educators.* http://schottfoundation.org/sites/default/files /restorative-practices-guide.pdf.

Neff, Kristin. 2016. "Don't Fall into the Self-Esteem Trap: Try a Little Self-Kindness." *Mindful,* February 17. http://www.mindful.org /dont-fall-into-the-self-esteem-trap-try-a-little-self-kindness.

Ochshorn, Susan. 2015. *Squandering America's Future: Why ECE Policy Matters for Equality, Our Economy, and Our Children.* New York: Teachers College Press.

Palmer, Parker J. 1998. "Thirteen Ways of Looking at Community (. . . with a Fourteenth Thrown in for Free)." *Inner Edge,* August/September. www .couragerenewal.org/parker/writings/13-ways-of-looking-at-community.

Pearce, Craig L., and Jay A. Conger. 2003. "All Those Years Ago: The Historical Underpinnings of Shared Leadership." In *Shared Leadership: Reframing the Hows and Whys of Leadership,* edited by Craig L. Pearce and Jay A. Conger, 1–18. Thousand Oaks, CA: Sage Publications.

Petrie, Nick. 2014. *Future Trends in Leadership Development.* www.ccl.org /wp-content/uploads/2015/04/futureTrends.pdf.

Pink, Daniel H. 2009. *Drive: The Surprising Truth about What Motivates Us.* New York: Riverhead Books.

Preskill, Stephen, and Stephen D. Brookfield. 2009. *Learning as a Way of Leading: Lessons from the Struggle for Social Justice.* San Francisco: Jossey-Bass.

Prochaska, James O., and Carlos C. DiClemente. 1983. "Stages and Processes of Self-Change of Smoking: Toward an Integrative Model of Change." *Journal of Consulting and Clinical Psychology* 51 (3): 390–95.

Raelin, Joseph A. 2003. *Creating Leaderful Organizations: How to Bring Out Leadership in Everyone.* San Francisco: Berrett-Koehler.

Rath, Tom. 2015. *Are You Fully Charged? The 3 Keys to Energizing Your Work and Life.* Arlington, VA: Silicon Guild.

Rock, David, and Jeffrey Schwartz. 2006. "The Neuroscience of Leadership." *Strategy+Business,* May 30. www.strategy-business.com /article/06207?gko=6da0a.

Schein, Edgar H. 2011. *Helping: How to Offer, Give, and Receive Help.* San Francisco: Berrett-Koehler.

———. 2013. *Humble Inquiry: The Gentle Art of Asking Instead of Telling.* San Francisco: Berrett-Koehler.

Schumann, Mary Jean. 2013. Foreword to *Early Childhood Education for a New Era: Leading for Our Profession* by Stacie Goffin, xi–xiv. New York: Teachers College Press.

Senge, Peter M. 1990. *The Fifth Discipline: The Art and Practice of the Learning Organization.* New York: Currency.

Senge, Peter, Hal Hamilton, and John Kania. 2015. "The Dawn of System Leadership." *Stanford Social Innovation Review,* Winter: 27–33. www.ssireview.org/articles/entry/the_dawn_of_system_leadership.

Sykes, Maurice. 2014. *Doing the Right Thing for Children: Eight Qualities of Leadership.* St. Paul, MN: Redleaf Press.

Tenney, Lauren. 2016. "Next Stage for Self-Management: Skilled Facilitator Training." *Enlivening Edge,* September 6. www.enliveningedge.org/tools-practices/next-stage-self-management-skilled-facilitator-training.

Tschannen-Moran, Megan. 2004. *Trust Matters: Leadership for Successful Schools.* San Francisco: Jossey-Bass.

Twist, Lynne. 2006. *The Soul of Money: Reclaiming the Wealth of Our Inner Resources.* New York: W. W. Norton.

Uhl-Bien, Mary, Russ Marion, and Bill McKelvey. 2007. "Complexity Leadership Theory: Shifting Leadership from the Industrial Age to the Knowledge Era. *Leadership Quarterly* 18 (4): 298–318.

US Department of Education. 2013. *For Each and Every Child—A Strategy for Education Equity and Excellence.* www2.ed.gov/about/bdscomm/list/eec/equity-excellence-commission-report.pdf.

Wheatley, Margaret, and Debbie Frieze. 2010. "Leadership in the Age of Complexity: From Hero to Host." www.margaretwheatley.com/articles/Leadership-in-Age-of-Complexity.pdf.

Whitebook, Marcy, Caitlin McLean, and Lea J. E. Austin. 2016. *Early Childhood Workforce Index.* Berkeley: Center for the Study of Child Care Employment, University of California–Berkeley. http://cscce.berkeley.edu/files/2016/Early-Childhood-Workforce-Index-2016.pdf.

Wiseman, Liz. 2010. *Multipliers: How the Best Leaders Make Everyone Smarter.* With Greg McKeown. New York: HarperCollins.

W. K. Kellogg Foundation. 2007. *The Collective Leadership Framework: A Workbook for Cultivating and Sustaining Community Change.* http://www.ethicalleadership.org/uploads/2/6/2/6/26265761/collective_leadership_framework_workbook.pdf.

# Index